D0891548

Individual Goals and Organizational Objectives

A Study of Integration Mechanisms

JON H. BARRETT

Center for Research on Utilization of Scientific Knowledge

Institute for Social Research
The University of Michigan
Ann Arbor, Michigan

Library of Congress Catalog Card Number: 77-632403

Printed by Braun-Brumfield, Inc.
Ann Arbor, Michigan

Manufactured in the United States of America

Acknowledgments

This study owes its existence to a number of persons besides its official author, and I would like to acknowledge here the special contributions of a few of these persons.

Several colleagues at The University of Michigan facilitated my work by their suggestions and assistance. The general topic was suggested by David Bowers, and he served as a sounding board as I broadened and elaborated the idea into its present form. Arnold Tannenbaum helped clarify my thinking on basic issues of concept definition by periodically asking some troublesome questions. Frank Andrews was an invaluable resource regarding methodological issues and analysis procedures. Ed Lauman improved the breadth of the analysis by emphasizing the importance of demographic variables. Stanley Seashore smoothed administrative procedures and provided detailed editorial reviews of various drafts. Each of these contributions improved the quality of the product without seriously complicating my execution of the research. They each have my thanks.

Financial support for the study came from three sources—the Office of Naval Research (Contract number N00014-67-A-0181-0013), The Business Administration Foundation at the University of Texas, and basic research funds of the Business and Industry Group in the Center for Research on Utilization of Scientific Knowledge (CRUSK) at The University of Michigan's Institute for Social Research. I am grateful to each of these institutions for the indispensable resources they provided to support this research.

The present study made extensive use of data collected as part of a large multi-organization longitudinal research program being conducted by the Business and Industry Group mentioned above. Without the questionnaire instrument, field site resources and data processing programs developed by this group, my study would have been much more difficult to execute. Many persons in this group provided assistance to me during the course of this study and their help is greatly appreciated.

George Mylonas and Mauricio Font from the CRUSK data processing staff served as my link to the computer and efficiently executed much of the data processing and analysis required by this work. Jim Taylor also helped speed the data processing by answering my many questions on procedural matters.

Mrs. Elaine Watson performed not only the considerable volume of typing required through various drafts and revisions, but also handled numerous errands and administrative details for an absentee author.

Joyce Kornbluh, CRUSK's very able editor, provided a thorough review of the final manuscript and efficiently managed its conversion into printed form.

John Thomas, director of the larger refinery study which provided the data for this research, was for me an especially valuable mixture of colleague and friend during the period when this study was in process. He helped me sort out a variety of pressures into a workable set of priorities.

Finally, I would like to say a special thank-you to Pat, Sheryl, and Joyce who lived through much work-generated turmoil with me and helped make this sometimes difficult period one of significant personal growth as well as professional development.

TABLE OF CONTENTS

Page

LIST OF TABLES

LIST OF FIGURES

ix

1
The Problem and a Theoretical Framework

The Problem

This study is concerned with an aspect of one of the most basic issues in social theory and practice—the nature of the relationship between individual human beings and social organizations. As with most basic issues, this question is not a new one. It was presented in general terms rather well two centuries ago by Jean Jacques Rousseau:

> The problem is to find a form of association which will defend and protect with the whole common force the person and good of each associate, and in which each, while uniting himself with all, may still obey himself alone, and remain as free as before. This is the fundamental problem (1949).

Organizational theorists writing in the early part of the present century presented the issue in somewhat more specific terms. Chester Barnard, in developing a theory of organizations as cooperative systems, stated the problem as one of providing for both "effectiveness"—attaining the objective or purpose of the cooperative system—and "efficiency"—satisfying the individual motives of the persons participating in the system (1938, pp. 33, 34). In a similar vein, Roethlisberger and Dickson, generalizing from their research experiences at the Western Electric Company, suggested that

> ... management has two major functions: (1) the function of securing the common economic purpose of the total enterprise, and (2) the function of maintaining the equilibrium of the social organization so that individuals through contributing their service to this common purpose obtain personal satisfactions that make them willing to cooperate (1939, p. 569).

Contemporary organization theorists continue to be concerned with this same issue, posed as a question by Chris Argyris:

> ...How is it possible to create an organization in which the individual may obtain optimum expression and, simultaneously, in which the organization itself may obtain optimum satisfaction of its demands? (1957, p. 24)

The International Congress of Applied Psychology in 1961 devoted a symposium to the issue of the relation of the individual to the system. In his introductory remarks to this symposium, Morris Viteles outlined the basic problem as one of

> ...how people can learn to work together in a manner which will simultaneously satisfy their needs and the objectives of the organization in which they find themselves (Viteles, Wilson, and Hutte, 1962, p. 97).

In his 1961 presidential address to the American Psychological Association's Division of Industrial Psychology, Raymond Katzell listed organizational factors needing research in order to determine what kinds of organizational policies and practices will work best. One of these factors is, "The degree of congruence or disparity between the goals of the organization and [those] of its employees (1962, p. 106)."

It appears, then, that the relationship between individuals and organizations—or, more specifically, the relation of an organization's objectives to the goals of its individual members—is an issue of both historical and current importance.

While the problems of integrating individual goals with organizational objectives have been frequently discussed, there are very few empirical studies which deal directly with this issue. In the development of general theoretical positions, considerable work has been done toward documenting the extent to which the structures and processes of most modern organizations are in conflict with the needs of healthy individual human beings (Argyris, 1957, 1964). Much work has been done, also, toward integrating the results of studies concerned with conditions and processes which differentiate more effective from less effective organizations in terms of achieving their objectives (Likert, 1961). Much of this integrative theoretical work has important implications for the problem of relating organizational objectives to individual goals, including the suggestion that some structures and processes may contribute to organizational effectiveness while at the same time being compatible with individual satisfaction and fulfillment. The focus of most empirical studies, however, has usually been *either* on conditions leading to organizational effectiveness *or* on conditions leading to individual satisfaction and fulfillment in organizations. Few empirical studies have concerned themselves directly with understanding conditions conducive to *simultaneously* satisfying individual needs and achieving organizational objectives, or with the consequences of such conditions for individual and organizational functioning. It is this latter focus which we wish to pursue in the present study. In the remainder of this monograph, we will present a theoretical framework for thinking about this issue and use the framework as a basis for exploring the issue empirically.

A Theoretical Framework

The theoretical framework to be presented here is concerned with a number of approaches used in organizations to integrate the goals of individuals with the objectives of the organization. In exploring these various approaches, we are assuming that organization administrators attach some importance to achieving such a state of integration and that they use or encourage the use of various strategies for achieving goal integration. There is some disagreement among organization theorists regarding whether a state of high integration of individual needs with organizational objectives is possible to achieve or whether it is desirable even if attainable (Etzioni, 1964; Leavitt and Whisler, 1958; Simon, 1960). We will not address this issue directly except to assert that some minimal level of integration would appear to be necessary for an organization to exist, if membership is at all voluntary. To the extent that organization administrators are concerned with achieving any given level of goal integration, the approaches they use to achieve this state can be a subject for investigation.

We define an organizational *objective* as any state of affairs (including both static and dynamic states) which contributes to the creation of an organization's primary outputs or to the fulfillment of its purposes or functions. An individual *goal* is any state of affairs (dynamic or static) which contributes to the fulfillment of an individual's needs, motives or desires. Organization members spontaneously commit themselves to the pursuit of individual *goals.* They do not necessarily commit themselves spontaneously to the pursuit of organizational *objectives.* An important problem for organization theorists and administrators, therefore, is to conceive mechanisms through which goals and objectives can be integrated, so that the same actions on the part of an organization member can lead to the attainment of both his personal goals and the organization's objectives. Organizations or sub-units whose members find it easy to attain both personal goals and organizational objectives through the activities they engage in as members of the organization may be said to have a high degree of *goal integration.*

Figure 1 presents these concepts schematically. $\underline{A}$ is the set of states or activities which contribute to the fulfillment of the individual's needs or motives. $\underline{B}$ is the set of states or activities which contribute to the creation of the organization's primary outputs. $\underline{C}$ is a subset of states or activities contributing both to the fulfillment of the individual's motives and to the creation of the organization's outputs. The degree of goal integration present may be thought of in terms of the size of subset $\underline{C}$ relative to the size of sets $\underline{A}$ and $\underline{B}$.

Three Goal Integration Models

Approaches to increasing the degree of goal integration in an organization—to increasing the size of subset $\underline{C}$ in Figure 1—may be classified into three broad, goal integration models, each encompassing a number of specific integration mechanisms.

The Exchange Model

Under this model, a fairly explicit bargaining relationship prevails between the organization and the individual. The organization offers the individual incentives presumed to be related to his personal goals and, in return, the individual devotes some of his time and energy to helping the organization achieve its objectives. A somewhat stronger characterization of this model is achieved by describing it as a conditional reinforcement model—the organization contributes to an individual's pursuit of personal goals on the condition and to the extent that he contributes to the achievement of the organization's objectives. One further feature of this approach can be communicated by characterizing it as an extrinsic reward model—what the organization does for the individual makes no direct contribution to the pursuit of its objectives, and what the individual does for the organization makes no direct contribution to the pursuit of his goals. In a strict sense, then, the exchange model is concerned more with ways of *relating* personal goals and organizational objectives than with ways of *integrating* them. It is assumed that only a minimal level of goal integration, as we have defined that term, is possible, and that to relate goals and objectives more closely than this limited integration allows requires that individual goal attainment be made conditional upon the achievement of organizational objectives.

The exchange model is presented schematically in Figure 2. In terms of this figure, the exchange model assumes that subset $\underline{C}$ will always be small relative to $\underline{A}$ and $\underline{B}$. Thus, this model does not call for an attempt to increase the size of $\underline{C}$, but instead calls for the individual and the organization to engage in an exchange of elements in sets $\underline{A}$ and $\underline{B}$. It can be thought of as attempting to create a subset $\underline{C}'$ by juxtaposing elements from sets $\underline{A}$ and $\underline{B}$ that are involved in exchange relationships between the individual and the organization.

Specific mechanisms falling under the exchange model can be differentiated in terms of the kind of incentives the organization offers the individual in return for his contribution to achieving its objectives:

Pay. One way of encouraging individuals to perform tasks that are

GOAL INTEGRATION

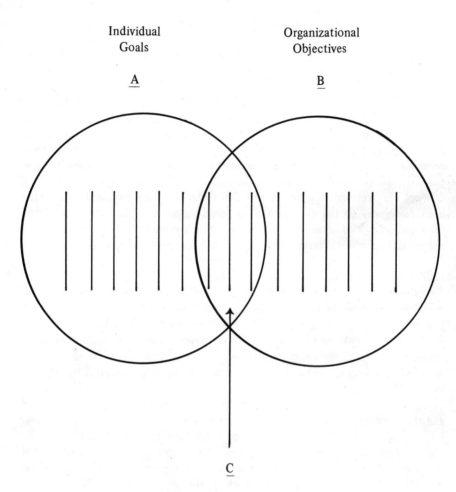

Extent of Goal Integration

Figure 1

related to organizational objectives but not to their personal goals is to offer them money in exchange for the performance of such tasks. Receiving money is assumed to be a personal goal for most individuals.

Informal social relations. In addition to material incentives such as pay, the organization may offer certain social incentives to the individual in exchange for his contributions to the achievement of organizational objectives. Examples of such social incentives include (1) considerate treatment from superiors, and (2) opportunities to engage in informal social relationships with peers.

A number of organization theorists have tended to view individual-organization relationships in terms of economic exchange, and thus may be said to emphasize the exchange model of goal integration. Much of the organization theory of Max Weber (1947), for example, makes use of general economic concepts, including the concept of exchange, and he tended to view relationships between organizations and individuals in terms of this exchange concept. In Weber's view, in return for material goods (primarily pay), the individual gives to the organization a certain amount of his undifferentiated time and energy to be used in the organization's productive activities. Once an individual accepts the terms of such an exchange, goal integration is assumed to be at an adequate level and the employee's subsequent behavior is explained by other concepts, primarily the concept of "legitimate authority."

Frederick Taylor (1923), founder of the "scientific management" movement, placed great emphasis on the use of a piecework incentive system of pay that would closely tie an employee's earnings to his level of production. He wanted to make the conditional relationship between the achievement of organizational objectives and the fulfillment of individual goals (conceived as a desire for money) more explicit and immediate than that implied by Weber's view.

The "inducements-contributions theory" developed by Chester Barnard and Herbert Simon also appears to emphasize an exchange model of goal integration. According to Simon, "To understand how the behavior of the individual becomes a part of the system of behavior of the organization, it is necessary to study the relationship between the personal motivation of the individual and the objectives toward which the activity of the organization is oriented (1957, p. 16)." Elsewhere, he summarizes his view of this relationship as follows:

> In the motivational theory formulated by Barnard and me, it is postulated that the motives of each group of participants can be divided into *inducements* (aspects of participation that are desired by the participants) and *contributions* (aspects of participation that are inputs into the organization's production function but that generally have negative utility to the participants). Each participant is motivated to maximize,

THE EXCHANGE MODEL

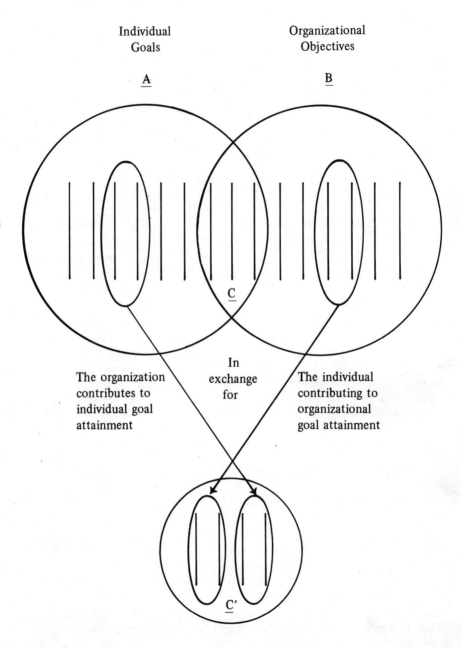

Individual
Goals

Organizational
Objectives

<u>A</u>

<u>B</u>

<u>C</u>

The organization
contributes to
individual goal
attainment

In
exchange
for

The individual
contributing to
organizational
goal attainment

<u>C</u>′

Figure 2

or at least increase his inducements while decreasing his contributions, and this motivation is a crucial consideration in explaining the decision to join (or remain). But "joining" means accepting an organizational role, and hence we do not need any additional motivational assumptions beyond those of inducements-contributions theory to explain the ensuing role-enacting behavior (1964).

Simon seems to be similar to Weber in assuming that a simple exchange model is adequate to explain the integration of individual motives and organizational objectives. They become integrated as soon as the individual agrees to join the organization, and this is determined by the acceptability of the "exchange" involving his undifferentiated time and effort, and payoffs in the form of wages and other incentives offered by the organization.

Explicit suggestions that such social incentives as considerate treatment from superiors or opportunities for informal interaction with peers should be used in the kind of conditional reward paradigm implied by our exchange model are not found in the writings of the best known organization theorists. Early writers in the "human relations" tradition (e.g., Roethlisberger and Dickson, 1939) pointed to the importance of such social incentives to the satisfaction of workers, and thus may be said to have raised the possibility that such incentives could be used in the same way as economic rewards. Some critics of human relations theory suggest that managers seized upon this possibility and actually used the ideas of human relations theorists as justification for substituting expressions of affection and symbols of prestige for increases in wages (Bendix and Fisher, 1961). While this appears to be more a criticism of managerial practice than of the ideas of human relations writers, it does indicate that the use of social incentives as an exchange mechanism can be seen as an extrapolation from existing organization theories.

The Socialization Model

This model is basically a social influence model, goal integration being achieved through influence processes which encourage the individual to value activities which help to achieve organizational objectives, or to disvalue activities which do not help achieve objectives. Through the use of persuasion or modeling behavior, the individual may be encouraged to adopt as personal goals some of the organization's objectives. This might be referred to as positive socialization. Similarly, the individual may be encouraged to give up some personal goals that conflict or interfere with the achievement of objectives, and this might be called negative socialization.

The socialization model is presented schematically in Figure 3. Here, subset $\underline{C}$ is enlarged, relative to sets $\underline{A}$ and $\underline{B}$, by moving the boundary of set $\underline{A}$ so that it comes to include elements which formerly existed only in set $\underline{B}$ (positive socialization). At the same time, some elements formerly in set $\underline{A}$

THE SOCIALIZATION MODEL

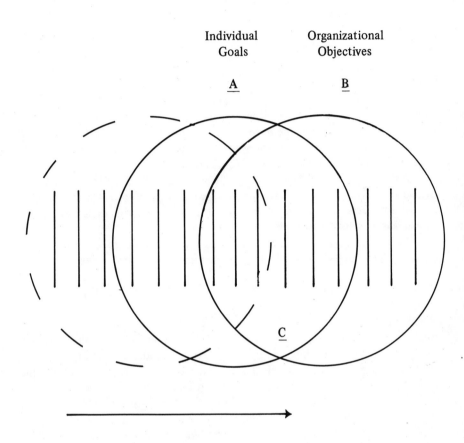

Figure 3

may now fall outside the boundary and no longer belong to that set (negative socialization). These two types of socialization need not occur together—an individual's repertoire of personal goals is not a fixed quantity. In terms of Figure 3, it is possible to conceive of the boundary of set A being stretched to include more elements from set B without dropping any elements already in set A.

Some specific socialization mechanisms can be differentiated in terms of the agent of socialization:

Leader socialization. In this mechanism a formal leader, by example and utterance, clearly indicates what the organizational objectives are, stresses their importance, and calls for them to be pursued with diligence. It is assumed that if a leader behaves in these ways his followers will come to value the objectives and will adopt them as personal goals.

Peer socialization. The kind of behavior described above can be performed by peers relating to each other as well as by a formal leader relating to his followers. When peers behave this way toward each other, the mechanism may be called peer socialization.

Edgar Schein (1961, 1967) describes organizational socialization as an influence process through which an individual learns the values, goals and norms of an organization. Involved in this process is a negative aspect in which the individual is confronted with a series of events, called "up-ending experiences," which serve the function of undoing old values so that the person will be prepared to learn new ones. The positive aspect of organizational socialization involves the individual's acquiring of new values from a variety of sources, including examples set by key models in the organization, instructions given to him directly by a trainer or employer, and the example of peers who have been in the organization longer. Although Schein is concerned primarily with the induction of new members into an organization and deals with a broader range of learnings than we are focusing on here, it is easy to recognize in his description of organizational socialization our concepts of positive and negative socialization and our distinction between leaders and peers as socialization agents.

The use of leader and peer socialization mechanisms is advocated in the organization theory of Rensis Likert (1967). He stresses the importance of a formal leader maintaining high standards of performance and using group methods of supervision. By maintaining high performance standards himself, the leader encourages subordinates to follow his example and set high standards for themselves. By using group methods of supervision, including group participation in setting performance objectives, the leader encourages the establishment of a group norm of high performance. Having accomplished this, the leader can then rely on the persuasive and modeling behavior of peers to supplement his own socialization activities. Thus, he increases the amount of influence that is brought to bear to encourage the individual to adopt personal goals that are in line with the high performance objectives of the organization.

Bowers and Seashore (1966), in their four-factor theory of leadership, describe one factor, which they call "goal emphasis," as behavior which stimulates an enthusiasm for meeting a group's goals or achieving excellent performance. They point out that goal-emphasizing behaviors may be engaged in either by formal leaders or by peers relating to each other, and present data indicating that such behavior is related to measures of organizational effectiveness. In this sense, they can be said to advocate the use of leader and peer socialization mechanisms to increase organizational effectiveness.

Blake and Mouton (1964) in their description of the "9,9" managerial style, which combines high concern for production with high concern for people, stress the importance of gaining understanding and acceptance by subordinates of the organization's purpose(s). The profit concept and cost consciousness are discussed as important aspects of organization purpose. Understanding and agreement regarding organization purposes are achieved through educational processes making substantial use of group discussion techniques to generate group commitment to organization objectives. According to Blake and Mouton, "The managerial skills needed at this point are ones of communication, decision-making and other attributes which aid individuals to get with it and embrace personal accomplishment goals which are consistent with organizational objectives (p. 151)." It seems clear from their discussion of "9,9" management that these authors advocate the use of leader and peer socialization mechanisms as means of achieving goal integration.

The Accommodation Model

In this model, emphasis is placed on taking individual goals into account in determining organizational objectives or designing procedures for attaining them. The needs and motives of the individual are taken as given, and the organization is structured and operated in such a way that the pursuit of organizational objectives will be intrinsically rewarding and will provide for the simultaneous pursuit of the individual's existing goals.

This model is presented schematically in Figure 4, which indicates that subset C is enlarged by moving the boundary of set B so that it comes to include elements which formerly existed only in set A. We might call this positive accommodation. At the same time, some elements formerly in set B may now fall outside the boundary and no longer belong to that set. This represents a situation in which the organization gives up an objective or activity because its pursuit will not help the individual attain any of his personal goals, and we might refer to this as negative accommodation.

Two specific accommodation mechanisms appear frequently in the recent writings of organization theorists:

Role or job design. The many specific activities required to achieve any given set of organizational objectives may be divided and assigned to individual members in a wide variety of ways. In this mechanism, the focus is on designing the individual's job or role so that it includes the kind, number and variety of activities required in the pursuit of his personal goals.

Participation. In this mechanism, individual members at all levels are included in a wide range of the objective-setting, problem-solving, and decision-making activities of the organization. Participation in these activities is held to contribute to goal integration in two ways. First, the process of participating will be directly satisfying to individuals whose personal goals include exerting control or contributing to policy formulation. Secondly, participation allows the individual to represent his own unique needs and interests in the processes which actually define the nature of the organization. The outcome should be solutions, decisions and objectives which have built into them provisions for attaining individual goals.

A number of current organization theorists emphasize the use of accommodation mechanisms as preferred means of integrating individual goals with organizational objectives.

Frederick Herzberg (1966), calling for "job enrichment" as the best way to motivate employees, illustrates the advocacy of role design as an accommodation mechanism. In applying the job enrichment concept, primary emphasis is placed on designing the content of jobs so that they match the individual employee's needs for interesting, challenging work.

Chris Argyris (1964) also gives considerable attention to the design of jobs or roles in specifying the characteristics of his system model of effective organization. He suggests using personality theory, which deals with the needs and abilities of persons, as a starting point for determining how jobs should be designed, and suggests numerous ways of enlarging roles to accommodate organizational structure and process to the individual's needs for "doing," "knowing" and "feeling."

McGregor (1960) persistently argues that the individual should be given opportunities to actively participate in processes which affect his work life. Included among these processes are performance appraisal, which becomes a collaborative review and goal-setting relationship between superior and subordinate, participation on problem-solving committees, such as those used in Scanlon-Plan companies to generate ideas for improving work procedures, and even participation in salary review and promotion decisions.

In emphasizing the use of group methods of supervision in which the supervisor involves his work group in solving work-related problems, and the wide distribution of decision-making throughout all levels of the organization, Likert (1961) also advocates the use of participation as an accommodation mechanism.

THE ACCOMMODATION MODEL

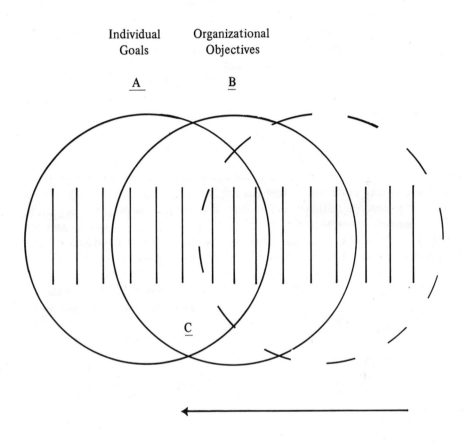

Figure 4

In discussing the democratic alternative to the traditional pyramid of organization structure, Katz and Kahn (1966) distinguish between executive power (policy implementation) and legislative power (policy formulation). The democratic structure, which these authors tend to favor, calls for a wide distribution of legislative power throughout the organization, seen in such practices as every member of the organization having a vote in the selection of the top executive, and the membership as a whole having veto power over any policy decision made in the organization. These suggestions for democratizing organizations may also be seen as an example of the use of participation as an accommodation mechanism.

Diagram of the General Theoretical Model

In Figure 5, we present a general theoretical model which relates the major concepts discussed in this chapter to each other and to concepts regarding some organizational and individual consequences of goal integration. This figure indicates that the three sets of goal integration mechanisms we have been discussing are conceived as processes which affect the degree of goal integration achieved in an organization. The degree of goal integration present is, in turn, conceived as affecting the quality of the organization's functioning, and the way in which individuals react to their membership in the organization. This general theoretical model served to guide the empirical study to be presented in the remainder of this monograph.

Figure 5

DIAGRAM OF THE GENERAL THEORETICAL MODEL

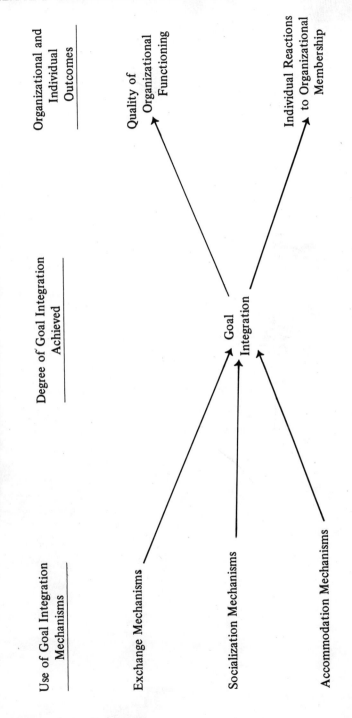

Use of Goal Integration Mechanisms

Exchange Mechanisms

Socialization Mechanisms

Accommodation Mechanisms

Degree of Goal Integration Achieved

Goal Integration

Organizational and Individual Outcomes

Quality of Organizational Functioning

Individual Reactions to Organizational Membership

II
Major Hypotheses and
Exploratory Research Questions

In this chapter, a series of hypotheses and research questions will be presented which provide a bridge between the theoretical concepts and model developed in the preceding chapter and empirical data which were gathered to test the validity of these concepts and the model which connects them. In the first section of this chapter, we will outline some major hypotheses directly concerned with testing the validity of the theoretical model. Later, a set of research questions will be presented which deal with the concepts associated with the model but which are more exploratory in nature and not so amenable to statement in the form of hypotheses or specific predictions.

Major Hypotheses

General hypothesis 1. The degree of goal integration in an organization is significantly related to the quality of the organization's functioning and the reactions of individuals to their membership in the organization.

This general hypothesis is related to that part of the theoretical model which is pictured in the right-hand portion of Figure 5. It is concerned with the question of whether the concept of goal integration has any practical importance, i.e., does it have any predictive or explanatory power with regard to important organizational process or outcome variables? If it does not, then one might reasonably question the importance of trying to understand mechanisms which affect the degree of goal integration achieved in an organization. Three specific predictions relate this general hypothesis to the empirical data of this study:

17

Prediction 1-A.   Measures of the degree of goal integration present in departmental units will show significant positive relationships to measures of the quality of functioning of these units.

Prediction 1-B.   Measures of the degree of goal integration present in work group units will show significant positive relationships to measures of the quality of functioning of these units.

Prediction 1-C.   Measures of the degree of goal integration individual members perceive to exist between themselves and the organization will show significant positive relationships to measures of the reactions of these individuals to organizational membership.

Confirmation of these predictions should serve to establish the importance of goal integration as an explanatory concept and justify further investigation into conditions which might be considered antecedents of goal integration.

General hypothesis 2.   The use of goal integration mechanisms associated with the exchange, socialization and accommodation models is significantly related to the degree of goal integration achieved in an organization.

This second general hypothesis relates to that part of the theoretical model pictured in the left-hand portion of Figure 5. It is concerned with the question of whether the mechanisms isolated by the model have any predictive or explanatory power with regard to the concept of goal integration. Three specific predictions relate this general hypothesis to empirical data collected in this study:

Prediction 2-A.   Measures of the use of *exchange* mechanisms within organizational units will show significant positive relationships to measures of the degree of goal integration present in these units.

Prediction 2-B.   Measures of the use of *socialization* mechanisms within organizational units will show significant positive relationships to measures of the degree of goal integration present in these units.

Prediction 2-C.   Measures of the use of *accommodation* mechanisms within organizational units will show significant positive relationships to measures of the degree of goal integration present in these units.

Confirmation of these predictions will establish the goal integration mechanism concepts as useful ones in the attempt to understand organizational processes which lead to a high level goal integration.

General hypothesis 3.   Goal integration mechanisms associated with the exchange, socialization and accommodation models are differentially effective in achieving high levels of goal integration. Specifically, *accommodation* mechanisms are more effective in this regard than *socialization* mechanisms which, in turn, are more effective than *exchange* mechanisms.

This hypothesis regarding the differential effectiveness of mechanisms associated with the three goal-integration models is not explicit in the theoretical model presented in the preceding chapter, but the association of the three models with different normative organization theories and some dynamic characteristics of the mechanisms themselves seemed to imply such an ordering. First, advocacy of the use of exchange mechanisms to achieve goal integration tends to be associated with classical organization theories (e.g., Gulick and Urwick, 1937; Taylor, 1923; Weber, 1947), which have been criticized as being based on incomplete and inaccurate motivational assumptions (cf. Etzioni, 1964; Katz and Kahn, 1966; March and Simon, 1958), and whose prescriptions regarding effective management practices are therefore subject to some doubt. Advocacy of the use of socialization and accommodation mechanisms, on the other hand, tends to be characteristic of organization theories which explicitly claim to be based on more complete and more accurate motivational assumptions than classical theories (e.g., Argyris, 1964; Likert, 1961; McGregor, 1960), and whose prescriptions regarding effective management practices should therefore be more valid. Extending this line of thought to the present problem leads to the argument that exchange mechanisms, associated with the less complete and less accurate classical organization theories, will be less effective in achieving goal integration than socialization or accommodation mechanisms which are associated with more complete and more accurate organization theories. This line of reasoning supports that part of the above hypothesis which asserts that exchange mechanisms are the least effective of the three kinds. The argument that accommodation mechanisms are more effective than socialization mechanisms requires an examination of the differential dynamics of these two processes. The basic difference is that socialization mechanisms involve a process that is expected *gradually* to bring individual goals in line with organizational objectives,[1] whereas accommodation mechanisms involve the installation of processes whose *immediate effect* is expected to be greater goal integration. Thus, organizations using socialization mechanisms can be expected to be constantly *moving toward* greater goal integration, but organizations using accommodation mechanisms can be expected to *have achieved* a high level of goal integration. Similar reasoning regarding the more rapid results to be expected from situational or structural changes than from changes in the psychological makeup or behavior of persons is found in the work of Fred Fiedler on leadership (1967). He suggests that effective leadership is a function not only of the leader's behavior, but also of the situation in which the leader is placed. Fiedler argues, further, that it may be easier to achieve effective leadership by altering the situation to match the leader's existing style (i.e., by accommodating him) than by changing the leader to match the demands of the situation (i.e., by socializing him). Extending this line of reasoning to the present problem leads to the argument that accommodation mechanisms, which involve changing the situations which confront individuals, may be more effective in achieving goal integration than socialization mechanisms, which involve changing individuals themselves. This rather tortuous chain of reasoning, then, leads to the particular ordering of mechanisms which appears in the hypothesis presented above. The specific prediction which follows from this hypothesis is the following:

Prediction 3-A.   Measures of the use of *accommodation* mechanisms will show higher positive relationships to measures of goal integration than will measures of the use of *socialization* mechanisms. Measures of the use of *socialization* mechanisms will, in turn, show higher positive relationships to measures of goal integration than will measures of the use of *exchange* mechanisms.

The three general hypotheses presented above, and the specific predictions associated with them, constitute the major hypotheses of the present

---

[1]The concept of socialization is used in sociology and psychology to describe the gradual adoption by individuals of basic values and attitudes that are consonant with the requirements or prevailing norms of their society.

study. A number of additional issues were investigated, however, and these are outlined below in the form of exploratory research questions.

Exploratory Research Questions

The first general issue that seemed important to explore concerns the relationship of our goal integration measures to some general demographic characteristics and some organizationally determined characteristics of the subjects included in this study:

General question 1. To what extent is the degree of goal integration experienced by individuals a function of their standing on some general demographic characteristics or their location in the social structure of the organization?

Two more specific questions flow from this and can be explored through the use of data available in the present study:

Question 1-A. To what extent is the degree of goal integration experienced by individuals a function of their age, the amount of formal education they have had, or whether they grew up in a predominately rural or urban area?

Question 1-B. To what extent is the degree of goal integration experienced by individuals a function of their tenure with the organization, the kind of work they do, or their location in the hierarchical structure of the organization?

These questions could be important to the present study for two reasons. First, the discovery of some meaningful relationships between the kind of demographic variables mentioned above and our measures of goal integration could increase our confidence in the validity of the goal integration measures. A person's age, his level of education and the relative urbanness of his early environment may be considered indicators of the number and variety of experiences he has had in his life. These experiences, in turn, may be expected to affect his basic values and the personal goals he chooses to pursue. A person's location in the social structure of an organization, as indicated by his tenure, the kind of work he does, or his hierarchical level, might be expected to affect the kind of organizational objectives he is asked to pursue. Both the kind of personal goals an individual brings to an organization and the kind of organizational objectives he is asked to pursue should affect the extent to which he experiences goal integration as a member of the organization. Because of this, our confidence in the validity of the goal integration measures would be increased by the discovery that they show some relationship to at least some of these demographic variables.

On the other hand, if these demographic variables show very strong relationships to our measures of goal integration, then it might be argued that they provide a more adequate explanation of conditions that produce high levels of goal integration than do our concepts of goal integration mechanisms. These variables might, in other words, be considered as providing a rival hypothesis to our general hypothesis 2, which asserts that the degree of goal integration experienced by organization members is a function of the use of various goal integration mechanisms. The building of relatively sophisticated theoretical models which attempt to explain the process by which some social psychological phenomenon occurs is a legitimate scientific activity. If, however, there are less sophisticated models available which are more powerful in terms of their ability to account for the phenomenon under study, this fact should at least be acknowledged. Answering the two questions posed above should allow us to either refute or acknowledge this state of affairs as it applies to the present study.

In the general question presented above, we were concerned with demographic variables as possible *rival concepts* to the major independent variables of this study. In the following question, the concern is with whether these same demographic variables might *interact* with our independent variables in determining the level of goal integration achieved in an organization:

> *General question 2.*   Is the relationship between the use of particular goal integration models by an organizational unit and the degree of goal integration achieved affected by the general demographic characteristics of the unit's members or by the location of the unit in the general social structure of the organization?

A more specific question relates this general issue to the data of the present study:

> *Question 2-A.*   Are relationships between measures of the use of goal integration models and measures of the degree of goal integration achieved different for organizational units which differ in terms of the urban/rural origins of their members, in terms of the average tenure or educational level of their members, or in terms of the kind of work they perform, or

their location in the hierarchical structure of the organization?

These questions are of interest because they concern the generality of the major hypotheses of this study. It might be argued, for example, that the socialization model would be effective with persons of rural background who ascribe to middle-class norms concerning the virtue of hard work and responsibility to employer, but not with persons of more urban background who tend to be alienated from such middle-class norms ·(cf. Blood and Hulin, 1967). Similarly, it could be argued that the exchange model should be most effective at lower levels in the organization where employees are accustomed to a bargaining relationship with the organization through their affiliation with a labor union. Answering question 2-A above will allow us to determine whether whatever effectiveness the goal integration models are shown to have is general or whether their effectiveness depends in part on the kind of persons or organizational units to which they are applied.

A third general question concerns relationships among the use of different goal integration models or mechanisms:

General question 3. How do the various goal integration models or mechanisms relate to each other? Are the different models or mechanisms used together, or do they tend to serve as substitutes for one another?

This question was suggested by some writings of Rensis Likert concerning consistency within management systems (1967, pp. 116-123). His thesis is that certain kinds of organizational practices tend to go with certain others, and that these relationships among various practices provide the basis for differentiating management *systems*. For example, an organization which has a highly centralized decision-making system will tend to have a particular kind of communication system, namely a highly vertical one with orders and instructions flowing downward and performance reports flowing upward. An organization whose decision-making system is decentralized will have its own particular kind of communication system, in this case one in which information concerning objectives, performance and problems flows in all directions, upward, downward, and laterally. Such relationships among practices within organizations provide the basis upon which Likert differentiates autocratic from more participative management systems. With regard to the present study, this idea suggests the question of whether meaningful relationships might be found among the organization practices represented by our different goal integration models or mechanisms. For example, are the exchange, socialization and accommodation approaches to achieving goal integration all used together, thus implying that they might all be part of a single management system? Or does the use of one approach tend to be independent of, or negatively related to, the use of others, implying that these approaches may belong to different management systems? The following specific question addresses itself to this issue in terms of the data available in the present study:

> *Question 3-A.*   What are the relationships among summary measures of the use of the three goal integration models?

It also seemed appropriate to inquire about the relationships among particular mechanisms within each goal integration model. For example, is role design used along with participation in applying an accommodation approach to achieving goal integration, or does one mechanism tend to be used as a substitute for the other? Three specific questions in the present study are related to this issue:

> *Question 3-B.*   Within the exchange model, what is the relationship between the use of pay and the use of informal social relations as mechanisms?

> *Question 3-C.*   Within the socialization model, what is the relationship between the use of leader socialization and the use of peer socialization as mechanisms?

> *Question 3-D.*   Within the accommodation model, what is the relationship between the use of role design and the use of participation as mechanisms?

In the four questions presented above, we have been concerned with whether the various mechanisms or models tend to be used together or as substitutes for one another. In the following question, we are interested in what *effect* the simultaneous use of more than one mechanism or model has on the level of goal integration achieved:

> *General question 4.*   Is the simultaneous use of more than one model or mechanism associated with a higher level of goal integration than the use of any one model or mechanism alone?

Two specific questions growing out of this interest in the effect of using multiple approaches to achieving goal integration can be explored with the data available in this study:

Question 4-A.   Do measures of the use of exchange, socialization and accommodation models show a higher positive relationship to measures of goal integration when taken all together than any one does when taken by itself?

Question 4-B.   Within each goal integration model, do measures of the use of the particular mechanisms show a higher positive relationship to measures of goal integration when taken together than either one does when taken singly?

Answers to these questions may indicate whether we have isolated models and mechanisms that are independent from one another in terms of their ability to explain separate portions of the variance in goal integration. If measures of the use of models or mechanisms relate more highly to goal integration measures when taken together than when taken singly, then we may conclude that they are explaining non-overlapping portions of the variance in goal integration. If some of the individual measures relate to goal integration just as highly by themselves as they do when combined with other measures, then it might be argued that we have not isolated *different* processes leading to high levels of goal integration.

The next general question reflects a ubiquitous dichotomy which can be applied to discussions of practically every area of human affairs:

General question 5.   Within the three goal integration models, is it possible to distinguish "positive" and "negative" mechanisms which differ in the strength of their relationships to goal integration?

Some examples will indicate how the terms "positive" and "negative" are used here to draw distinctions between different approaches to achieving goal integration. In the application of an exchange model, for instance, it might be interesting to know whether the offering of an incentive as a *reward* for contributing to organization objectives has a different effect than the threat of withholding an incentive as a *punishment* for failure to contribute. With regard to the socialization model, one might ask whether inducing an individual to *adopt* some new personal goals that are in line with organizational objectives is more effective than trying to get him to *give up* some existing goals that conflict with organizational objectives. An analogous distinction may be drawn within the accommodation model between the organization *adopting* objectives or work methods that are congruent with individual goals and *abandoning* objectives or methods that conflict with individual goals. These issues will be explored through the following specific question:

Question 5-A.   Do measures of the use of "positive" mechanisms from the three goal integration models show higher positive relationships to measures of goal integration than do measures of the use of "negative" mechanisms from the three models?

Organization theorists have been criticized on occasion for failure to give adequate attention to individual differences in motivation (Blood and Hulin, 1967; Strauss, 1963; Vroom, 1960). In terms of the concepts employed in the present study, individual differences in motivation are reflected in differences among individuals in the importance ascribed to particular goals. Inclusion of the following question represents an attempt to avoid the above criticism in the present study:

General question 6.   Is the strength of a particular mechanism's relationship to goal integration affected by individual differences in the importance of the goal implicit in that mechanism?

For example, is the effectiveness of pay as an exchange mechanism a function of how important money is to the persons to whom this mechanism is being applied? Do differences in the strength of the desire to participate in group meetings influence the effectiveness of such meetings as an accommodation mechanism? This general issue will be explored by bringing our data to bear on this specific question:

Question 6-A.   Do measures of the use of particular goal integration mechanisms show higher positive relationships to measures of the degree of goal integration achieved for persons who assign great importance to the goals implicit in those mechanisms than they do for persons who ascribe lesser importance to these goals?

A final exploratory research question was suggested by some differences between two current articulations of exchange theory in sociology. George Homans builds his formulation of the process of social exchange from some basic concepts of behavioristic psychology and elementary economics (1958). Among the concepts borrowed from the behaviorists is the notion that making a reward *contingent* upon the display of some desired behavior will increase the likelihood of that behavior occurring. This same idea is implicit in the exchange model of goal integration which holds that the way to increase goal integration is to make the fulfillment of individual goals contingent upon the individual's contributing to the achievement of organizational objectives. In other words, the organization will contribute to fulfilling the individual's goals *if* the individual contributes to achieving the organization's objectives. In the next chapter, we will see that our measures of the use of an exchange model reflect this contingency relationship very clearly. Peter Blau, however, draws a distinction between this approach to exchange relationships, which he calls "economic exchange," and his concept of "social exchange" (1964, p. 93). In Blau's conception of the social exchange process, reciprocal obligations are generated by providing rewards with *no explicit conditions* attached. Adapting this approach to our concern with organization-individual relationships, we might say that the organization contributes to fulfilling the individual's goals, with no explicit conditions attached. This unconditional reward policy then generates reciprocal feelings of obligation on the part of the individual which lead him to contribute to achieving the organization's objectives. This approach to achieving goal integration still involves an exchange of organizational contributions to the fulfillment of individual goals for individual contributions to the attainment of organizational objectives, but the terms of the exchange are not made explicit. Blau's conception of social exchange was not used in formulating our concept of the exchange model because of the difficulty of differentiating its basic assumptions from those of our accommodation model, namely, that individual goals are accepted as given and organizational processes are designed so that they can be fulfilled. Nevertheless, the difference between the Homans and Blau conceptions seemed to pose some interesting questions regarding the effects of conditional versus unconditional provision of incentives. Accordingly, we included in the present study measures of the unconditional provision of incentives as well as the measures of conditional provision of incentives which were used to operationalize our exchange model of goal integration. These two sets of measures will be used to examine the following general question:

General question 7.   Does the conditional provision of incentives, implicit in the exchange model, differ from the unconditional provision of incentives in terms of the strength of its relationship to goal integration?

A more specific statement of this question, which connects it more closely to the data of this study, is:

Question 7-A.   Do measures of the use of exchange mechanisms show higher positive relationships to measures of goal integration than do measures of the unconditional provision of the same incentives used in those exchange mechanisms?

III
Methodology

Site and Sample

Subjects in this study are employees of a large, modern oil refinery located in an industrial city of about 100,000 population in the southern part of the United States. This refinery employs approximately 2,800 persons drawn predominately from the local area. The work force is fairly old and stable, predominately male, mostly rural in background, with a moderately high level of education for a manufacturing organization. About 40 per cent of the total work force is salaried, with the remaining 60 per cent classified as hourly wage earners.

The refinery is organized into 18 departments within three major divisions. There is a Processing Division concerned with operating the continuous-process refining equipment; a Maintenance Division concerned with maintaining existing equipment and constructing new facilities; and an Administrative Division comprised of technical research and development activities, staff groups and administrative services units. The Maintenance Division is the largest of the three, with 50 per cent of the employees, followed by Processing, with 29 per cent, and the Administrative Division, with 21 per cent.

Included in the present study are 1,781 of the refinery's employees, representing all major classifications of employees *except* the following: apprentices, who spend a considerable proportion of their work time in training activities; a small group of unskilled laborers, who perform janitorial and other miscellaneous chores; secretarial and stenographic employees, and employees who could not be classified into a work group unit having at least two subordinates reporting to the same supervisor. The three major divisions, all 18 departments, and every level of management are represented in this study. A more detailed description of the sample appears in Appendix A.

Measures

A 157-item paper-and-pencil survey questionnaire was administered to employees of the refinery in April, 1968. A 100 per cent coverage of the employees was attempted; the actual response rate achieved was 85 per cent. Measures used in the present study were constructed from a subset of the 157 items included in this questionnaire. Most individual questionnaire items are answered on a five-point Likert-type scale, with a standard set of answer alternatives. Measures of the major theoretical concepts being investigated in this study are presented in Appendix B in the same order in which they will appear in the discussion of results in the following chapter. A few additional measures will be introduced in the following chapter as they are needed for explaining the results of particular analyses.

Index Construction

Most of the measures used in this study are indices, constructed by combining in various ways the responses to selected single-item measures. The particular method used for combining single-item scores into index scores varies from one index to another. For most indices, the starting point was to assume that the mean of two or more single item scores was the desired index score. This seemed an appropriate starting assumption since, in most cases, the single items being combined into an index were considered alternate measures of a single concept. An examination of the correlations among items within these sets proved this to be a reasonable conclusion (see the first column of Table 1). Moreover, variances of the single-item distributions were roughly equal, due largely to the fact that nearly all items made use of a five-point response scale. Weighting of scores on the basis of differences in variance was, therefore, not indicated.

A disturbing characteristic of the distributions of several single-item measures, however, was their tendency to be negatively skewed, with a disproportionate number of responses falling near the upper end of the scale. A straightforward mean-score approach to index construction would have preserved this skewness characteristic in the index scores. It was decided, therefore, to use the indexing operation to correct for skewness in the individual items. In essence, this procedure involved examining the distribution of index scores that would result from a straightforward mean-score approach and, when such a distribution proved to be highly skewed, recoding index scores as they were constructed so that cases at the lower end of the scale would be combined and the total set of cases distributed more evenly over the range of possible index scores. A simple example will clarify the procedure. An index for an individual respondent, constructed by taking the mean score of two single items, each having five discreet response categories coded from one to five, could have any of the values indicated in the following table, depending on the combination of scores on the two items:

		Score on Item A				
		1	2	3	4	5
	1	1.0	1.5	2.0	2.5	3.0
Score	2	1.5	2.0	2.5	3.0	3.5
on	3	2.0	2.5	3.0	3.5	4.0
Item	4	2.5	3.0	3.5	4.0	4.5
B	5	3.0	3.5	4.0	4.5	5.0

An examination of the bivariate frequency distribution of individuals on these two items might reveal that 10 per cent of the index scores would fall in the 5.0 cell, 40 per cent would fall in the two 4.5 cells, another 40 per cent in the three 4.0 cells, with the remaining 10 per cent being scattered throughout the remaining cells. In such a case, we might leave the 5.0 cell with its present code value, recode the two 4.5 cells to 3.5, recode the three 4.0 cells to 2.5, and recode all the remaining cells to 1.0. This would result in a distribution of index scores having 10 per cent 1.0's, 40 per cent 2.5's, 40 per cent 3.5's, and 10 per cent 5.0's. This distribution would be symmetric about a mean of 3.0, with a range of 1.0 to 5.0.

Such a procedure is justifiable here because the primary analysis methods used in this study require only ordinal assumptions about the data, and none of the analysis or conclusions require a literal interpretation of particular response alternatives from the original questionnaire. Most of the index measures described in Appendix B were constructed by using either a straightforward mean-score approach or the adjusted mean-score procedure described above. Exceptions are described as they are presented in Appendix B.

Levels of Data Aggregation

Questionnaire data used in this study were prepared at three different levels of aggregation. At the individual level, there are measures on 1,781 employees who completed the questionnaire instrument. Every individual respondent has a score on each of the measures described in Appendix B.

The 1,781 individual employees fall into 233 work groups, each work group consisting of a number of employees who report to the same superior. Work group size ranges from 2 to 26 subordinates. There is a mode of 6 and a median of 5.92 subordinates per work group, with 88 per cent of the work groups having between 2 and 12 subordinates.

These same 1,781 individual employees can also be divided up in terms of their departmental affiliation. There are 18 departments ranging in size from 17 to 367 employees, with a median size of 78.5 employees. Half of the departments fall in the range of 50 to 100 employees.

All of the index measures described above were constructed at the individual level, and then aggregated by averaging index scores across the individuals who constitute the members of a particular work group or department. Each respondent has equal weight in all analyses performed at the individual level. Every individual also has equal weight within his work group or department in determining the score of that unit on measures used in this study. Analyses performed on data at the work group or department levels, however, give equal weight to each such *unit* included in the analysis, regardless of the number of respondents who belong to that unit.

Data at a particular level of aggregation are used when that level appears most appropriate for the analysis being performed. For example, when department functioning is being used as the dependent variable in an analysis, data aggregated at the department level is used. When the dependent variable involves individual reactions to the organization, data from the individual level is employed. For analyses concerned with the relationship between the use of particular goal integration mechanisms and the degree of goal integration achieved, it was decided to use data aggregated at the work group level. A number of factors influenced this decision. First, the number of work groups (233) was large enough to make this choice an acceptable one in terms of the simple criterion of number of cases. Secondly, while the concept of goal integration refers, at the most basic level, to the relationship between an individual and his organizational unit, the concept of goal integration *mechanisms* has as its most basic referent processes which characterize the organizational *unit* itself. Data at the work group level provide the best available sample of such organizational units. In addition, the use of work group means to measure the use of goal integration mechanisms provides measures based on the combined observations of more than one person. This provides more stable measures of the use of goal integration mechanisms than would responses of individuals. The group-mean measures are freer from measurement error and from the vagaries of individual perceptual distortion. If goal integration mechanisms are conceived as characterizing organizational units, then it is appropriate to use the general or average level of goal integration within a unit as the dependent variable. The mechanisms are expected to have a general effect on goal integration across individuals. If they do not, it may be because they are simply not effective mechanisms or because such mechanisms are not appropriately conceived as characterizing organizational units. Failure to find general effects across individuals within organizational units would constitute negative results for the present study, regardless of the underlying reason.

Distribution Characteristics of the Measures

A number of descriptive characteristics of the response distributions for the measures described earlier in this chapter are presented in Table 1. The first column of this table shows the product-moment correlations among the components that were combined to provide each index measure. These correlations were computed at the individual level because indices were constructed at that level. Most of these correlations are large enough to readily justify combining the components into a single index measure. Correlations of .18 and .14 among components of the goal integration and exchange model summary indices might cause some concern over the use of these summary measures. An examination of data from the analyses, however,, indicated that the summary index in most cases provided results as strong as, or stronger, than the results provided by either of the index components taken alone. This fact seems sufficient to justify use of these summary indices in the few cases where it proved more practical to do so. The relatively low correlation of .19 between the components of the influence distribution index is of little concern, since influence exercised by department heads and influence exercised by non-supervisory employees are not used here as duplicate measures of a single concept. The index is a difference score, representing the difference between measures of two different concepts, not an additive combination of two interchangeable measures of a single concept.

In the remaining columns of Table 1, descriptive moments of the response distributions are presented. In order, these are the mean, standard deviation, index of skewness and index of kurtosis. For most of these measures, the range of possible scores is from 1.00 to 5.00. The two exceptions are the influence distribution measure, which can range from −4.00 to 4.00, and goal integration index number one, which can range from 0.60 to 5.00. The level at which a set of measures will find its primary use in the analyses to be presented later is the level for which descriptive moments are presented here. For most measures, this is the work group level. Measures of departmental functioning and individual reactions are described at the department and individual levels of aggregation, respectively.

The information in Table 1 indicates that distribution characteristics of the measures used in this study adequately meet the requirements of the analysis procedures to be employed. These distributions are reasonably normal, symmetric about a mean which is close to the original questionnaire scale mean of 3.00, and not markedly peaked or flat-topped. The skewness and kurtosis indices for measures of department functioning and individual reactions deserve some brief comment. At the department level, these numbers must be interpreted with extreme caution, since it is seldom advisable to compute skewness and kurtosis measures for fewer than 100 cases (cf. McNemar, 1969, p. 27). They do suggest that skewness is within reasonable bounds, although it is greater here than with measures at the individual and work group levels. Distributions for the coordination and influence distribution measures are fairly peaked. Measures of individual reactions exhibit very little skewness, although they are somewhat more flat-topped than the other measures presented here. To correct for skewness in the original distributions at the individual level, it was necessary to combine some low-and middle-response categories and recode them with low-scale values, to balance the heavy concentration of cases which existed at the upper end of the scale. This resulted in distributions which are fairly rectangular in appearance, and this rectangular quality is reflected in the negative kurtosis indices for the satisfaction, commitment and health reaction measures. These departures from normal kurtosis shown by some of the department and individual level measures should not markedly affect the analysis procedures to be used with these data.

Some of the analysis procedures utilized in this study require that measures be in a categorical form rather than in the continuous form that we have been describing so far. For this purpose, the response distributions were collapsed into from three to five categories with roughly equal numbers of cases in each category. Most of the measures used in this study exist in two forms, continuous and categorical. Response distributions for the collapsed form of the measures are essentially rectangular due to the method used to construct categories. The analysis procedures using categorical measures make no assumptions about the form of these distributions, but the equal category frequencies characteristic of rectangular distributions are somewhat preferable to widely differing category frequencies.

Analysis Procedures

Most data collected by means of survey questionnaire instruments, including those used in this study, are basically ordinal in nature. Some of the most popular analysis techniques, on the other hand, are based on the assumption that the data to be analyzed meet interval measurement assumptions. An example of the latter is product-moment correlation, which further assumes that the relationship between any two variables being analyzed is linear in form. When it can be assumed that relationships are linear, and when response distributions are or can be made to be reasonably normal (as they were in this study), then product-moment correlation may be used with data that are basically ordinal in nature without seriously jeopardizing the results. Some limited use of this technique will be made in this study, primarily for practical reasons. Ready availability of computer programs for generating correlation coefficients makes this technique the most efficient one to use when measures of relationship among large numbers of variables are desired. This efficiency proved useful for some purposes in the present study and, as the previous

Table 1

MEASURES OF MAJOR CONCEPTS:
RELATIONSHIPS AMONG INDEX COMPONENTS AND
DESCRIPTIVE MOMENTS OF THE DISTRIBUTIONS

Major Concepts	Average r among Components*	Mean (E^1)	S.D. (E^2)	Skewness (E^3)	Kurtosis (E^4)
Goal Integration (N=233 groups)					
Index #1	.36	2.74	0.58	−0.08	0.08
Index #2	.44	3.55	0.46	−0.35	1.27
Summary index	.18	3.15	0.41	−0.09	−0.16
Exchange Mechanisms (N=233 groups)					
Pay	**	3.03	0.63	−0.01	−0.29
Informal social relations	.26	2.84	0.74	−0.08	−0.19
Summary index	.14	2.96	0.52	−0.01	−0.43
Socialization Mechanisms (N-233 groups)					
Leader	.70	2.96	0.74	0.08	−0.08
Peer	.57	3.44	0.43	−0.24	0.16
Summary index	.48	3.22	0.52	0.04	−0.27
Accommodation Mechanisms (N=233 groups)					
Role design	.43	2.70	0.50	−0.07	0.18
Participation	.42	2.87	0.58	−0.21	−0.02
Summary index	.50	2.81	0.49	−0.10	−0.19
Department Functioning (N=18 departments)					
Communication	.25	3.24	2.76	−0.51	1.75
Coordination	.58	3.13	2.21	−1.41	2.84
Total influence	.32	2.85	2.56	0.83	0.92
Influence distribution	.19	1.37	2.54	−1.30	4.42
Work Group Functioning (N=233 groups)					
Interaction	.40	3.39	0.44	−0.08	0.54
Coordination	.65	3.25	0.51	−0.33	−0.18
Innovation	.68	3.39	0.47	−0.22	−0.01
Effectiveness	.47	3.81	0.39	−0.31	0.20
Individual Reactions (N=1781 individuals)					
Motivation	.60	3.21	1.02	−0.42	−0.38
Satisfaction	.51	3.03	1.58	0.16	−1.46
Commitment	.62	3.03	1.46	−0.02	−1.12
Health	.48	3.12	1.63	0.20	−1.76

*All correlations are at the individual level, N=1781
**Single item measure

section indicated, the measures meet reasonably well the major requirement regarding normality of the response distributions.

For analyses related to the major hypotheses of this study, however, an analysis technique was desired that did not require interval measurement or assume linear relationships among variables. The technique chosen exists in the form of a computer program called Multiple Classification Analysis (MCA) (Andrews, Morgan and Sonquist, 1967). This program computes a measure of relationship between two variables called the correlation ratio or eta (η), which requires only nominal measurement of the variables and takes into account any curvilinearity that may exist in the relationship between variables. In addition to eta, the MCA program computes for any set of predictor variables (1) the relationship of each predictor to the dependent variable while controlling for the effects of the other predictors in the set (beta or β), and (2) the relationship to the dependent variable of all predictors taken together (R). This program requires that the predictor variables be in categorical form (the collapsed form of the measures described in the preceding section were used for this purpose), and that the dependent variable be continuous and not highly skewed. Data used in this study meet these requirements, and extensive use was made of the MCA program in the analyses to be presented later.

For some analyses, Kendall's tau was used as a measure of relationship between two variables (cf. McNemar, 1969). Computation of this measure uses data in ordinal form for both the predictor and the dependent variable. The tau statistic requires no assumptions regarding the nature of response distributions for either variable.

IV
Results

This chapter presents the results of data analyses related to the major hypotheses and exploratory research questions outlined in Chapter 2. First, we will examine data regarding the ability of demographic variables to explain the degree of goal integration experienced by organization members. Next, results related to the major hypotheses and predictions of this study will be presented. Finally, we will look at data relevant to the remaining exploratory questions spelled out in Chapter 2.

Demographic Variables and Perceived Goal Integration

Results of the multiple classification analysis relating perceived goal integration to some general demographic characteristics of the respondents in this study are presented in Table 2 and Figure 6. Data from individual respondents were used in both of the demographic analyses presented in this section in order to make maximum use of the available data. For the majority of our demographic variables, the individual is the most appropriate referent—groups do not go to school or have birthdays. The concept of goal integration also refers, at the most basic level, to an individual's relationship to his organization. To obtain the best assessment of the extent to which goal integration is a function of a person's standing on a number of demographic variables, it appeared desirable to use data at the individual level.

In Table 2, and the many similar tables that will be presented, the first column under each predictor variable contains the correlation ratio statistic, eta, indicating the strength of relationship between that predictor, taken by itself, and the dependent variable. The second column under each predictor presents the statistic beta, an estimate of the strength of relationship between the predictor and the dependent variable, after adjusting for the effects of all the other predictors included in the table. The next to the last column of the table presents the multiple correlation coefficient between the set of pre-

Table 2

RELATIONSHIP OF AGE, EDUCATION AND
COMMUNITY BACKGROUND OF RESPONDENTS
TO PERCEIVED GOAL INTEGRATION

N = 1,781 Individuals

Goal Integration Measures	Predictor Variables							
	Age		Education		Background		R	R^2
	η	β	η	β	η	β		
Index #1	.08*	.08	.12**	.14	.04	.07	.14**	.02**
Index #2	.03	.04	.16**	.16	.04	.04	.15**[1]	.02**
Summary Index	.07*	.06	.17**	.17	.04	.06	.17**	.03**

[1]Computation of multiple-R's by the Multiple Classification Analysis program includes a correction for degrees of freedom. Here, and in some of the tables which follow, this correction occasionally results in a multiple-R that is smaller than the largest individual predictor eta.

*p <.05
**p <.01

Figure 6

RELATIONSHIP OF AGE, EDUCATION AND COMMUNITY BACKGROUND OF RESPONDENTS TO PERCEIVED GOAL INTEGRATION

N = 1,781 Individuals

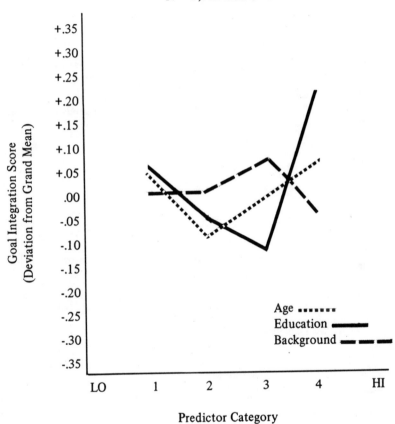

Predictor Category

dictors and the dependent variable. It indicates the strength of relationship between all the predictors taken together and the dependent variable. The last column contains the square of the multiple correlation coefficient and indicates the proportion of variance in the dependent variable which is explained by all the predictors taken together.

Figure 6, and the many similar figures which will appear in this chapter, present the results of the MCA graphically, which makes it possible to see the form of the relationship between each predictor and the dependent variable. The mean score on the dependent variable is plotted for each category of a given predictor variable. Since absolute scores on the dependent variable are not important to these analyses or their interpretation, dependent variable scores are expressed as deviations from the grand mean across all categories of the predictor.

Categories on the predictor variables for the present analysis are defined as follows:

Predictor Variable

	Age	*Education*	*Background*
	1 Under 41 years	Less than high school graduate	Rural area or farm
Predictor Category	2 41 - 45 years	High school graduate	Town or small city
	3 46 - 55 years	Some college	Suburban area near a large city
	4 Over 55 years	College graduate	Large city

From data presented in Table 2 and Figure 6, it is evident that the age, education and rural/urban background of the respondents included in this study show generally small and inconsistent relationships to our measures of the degree of goal integration they perceive to exist. These demographic characteristics, when taken together, explain only about 3 per cent of the variance in the summary goal integration measure, and this is due almost entirely to the education variable. We may dismiss age and rural/urban background as being essentially unrelated to our measures of goal integration. Education does show some relationship to our dependent variable, however, and the particular form of this relationship invites some speculative interpretation. The descending portion of the curve pictured in Figure 6 can be explained by the assertion that education develops in individuals value orientations and personal goals that are not easy to fulfill in the kind of industrial organizations that currently dominate our economy. Such assertions have been made by a number of current organization theorists (Argyris, 1964; Bennis, 1966; Blake and Mouton, 1964). The more education a person has, the more he develops these disparate values and goals, and the less likely he is to experience goal integration as a member of a typical industrial organization. This notion could explain the decrease in perceived goal integration with increasing education through "some college." It does not explain, however, the dramatic increase in goal integration that occurs as education increases to the level of college graduation. The most likely explanation for this ascending portion of the curve is related to the great symbolic value attached to college graduate status in our culture. It seems safe to assert that college graduates generally are able to get more attractive positions than non-graduates within any given organization. These positions are defined as more attractive precisely because they provide more opportunities for fulfilling individual goals. In the preceding chapter, it was asserted that goal integration is expected to vary as a function of the goals the individual brings to the organization and the kind of organizational objectives he is asked to pursue. The curvilinear relation of education to goal integration suggests that education is related to both of these factors. We might speculate that, up to the level of some college, education affects individual *goals* without substantially altering the kind of objectives individuals are asked to pursue. Within this range, individual goals become increasingly incongruent with the demands of available work roles. The achievement of college graduate status, however, significantly affects the kind of organizational *objectives* the individual is expected to work toward, these objectives being more congruent with the goals the individual brings to the organization.

With regard to exploratory question 1-A from Chapter 2, the data just presented seem to provide the following answer. The degree of goal integration experienced by individuals is not a function of their age or whether they grew up in a rural or urban area. It is affected to some extent by the amount of formal education they have had, but this effect is a complex one, not subject to a simple or straightforward interpretation.

Relationships of perceived goal integration to tenure, type of work performed and hierarchical level of respondents are presented in Table 3 and Figure 7. Definitions of the predictor categories are indicated below:

Predictor Variable

	Tenure	*Level*	*Function*
1	Under 5 years	Non-supervisory employees	Continuous process production
2	5-15 years	First-line supervisors	Mechanical maintenance and construction
3	16-25 years	Middle managers	Technical research and development
4	Over 25 years	Top managers	Staff and administration

As with the general demographic characteristics examined above, these organizationally determined characteristics of respondents show generally low relationships to our measures of goal integration. Taken together, tenure, hierarchical level and functional specialty of respondents account for only 5 per cent of the variance in our summary goal integration measure. The only variable in this set which shows a notable relationship to goal integration is hierarchical level, with a correlation ratio of .22. Hierarchical level has been shown in other studies to bear a significant positive relationship to the degree of fulfillment of individual needs (Porter, 1962; Porter and Lawler, 1966). We would expect individual need-fulfillment to show a positive relationship to our goal integration measures, since the fulfillment of individual needs is one of the two conditions required for a high level of goal integration to exist.

These data suggest the following answer to exploratory question 1-B from Chapter 2: the degree of goal integration experienced by individuals is not strongly related to their tenure with the organization or to the general nature of their work. It is affected somewhat by their location in the hierarchical structure of the organization, persons at higher levels being more likely to experience a high degree of goal integration than persons at lower levels in the hierarchy.

Overall results regarding the two sets of demographic variables just examined are reassuring in the context of the present study. The discovery of meaningful relationships between some of these variables and our measures of goal integration serves to increase our confidence in the validity of the latter measures. On the other hand, these demographic variables do not show such strong or consistent relationships to goal integration as to rival the major independent variables of this study in explaining conditions which produce

Table 3

RELATIONSHIP OF TENURE, HIERARCHICAL LEVEL AND
FUNCTIONAL SPECIALTY OF RESPONDENTS TO
PERCEIVED GOAL INTEGRATION

N = 1,781 Individuals

Goal Integration Measures	Predictor Variables									
	Tenure		Level		Function					
	η	β	η	β	η	β	R	R^2
Index # 1	.10**	.08	.23**	.23	.10**	.03	.23**	.06**
Index # 2	.03	.03	.12**	.14	.05	.06	.12**	.01**
Summary Index	.06	.06	.22**	.23	.08*	.04	.22**	.05**

*p <.05
**p <.01

Figure 7

RELATIONSHIP OF TENURE, HIERARCHICAL LEVEL AND
FUNCTIONAL SPECIALTY OF RESPONDENTS TO
PERCEIVED GOAL INTEGRATION

N = 1,781 Individuals

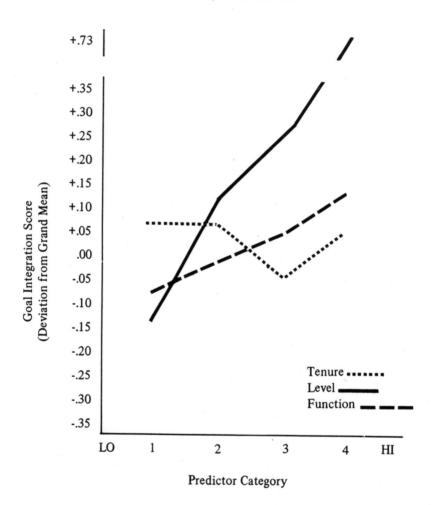

high levels of goal integration. Having established this fact, we can now proceed to present results related to the major hypotheses of the present investigation.

Goal Integration, Organizational Functioning, and Individual Reactions

Data to be presented in this section are related to general hypothesis 1 from Chapter 2, which asserts that the level of goal integration present in an organizational unit affects the functioning of that unit and the reactions of individual members to their participation in the organization. In the analyses presented in this section, decisions regarding the level of data aggregation to be used were based on the referent which appeared to be most appropriate to the dependent variables being considered. Thus, because the first analysis is concerned with measures of departmental unit functioning as dependent variables, data aggregated at the department level were used. In the next analysis, dependent variables refer to work group functioning, and data at the work group level is employed to assess the relationship of goal integration measures to these variables. Finally, when our interest is focused on individual reactions as dependent variables, we use data from individual respondents.

Prediction 1-A is partially confirmed by the data which appear in Table 4 and Figure 8, which indicate that our goal integration measures show some fairly high positive relationships to measures of the quality of functioning of departmental units in the refinery. While the degree of goal integration present in a departmental unit does not appear to bear any relation to the relative distribution of influence between the upper and lower levels within the department, it is strongly related to the exercise of influence by employees at all levels within the department. Goal integration, as measured by Index #1, is also strongly related to the adequacy of communication flow within departments and the adequacy of coordination between departments.

Results related to prediction 1-B appear in Table 5 and Figure 9. These data confirm the prediction of significant positive relationships between goal integration and work group functioning measures. The general level of interaction and the adequacy of coordination among work group members show the strongest relationships to goal integration scores, with multiple correlation coefficients of .27 and .31, respectively. Also related to goal integration, but somewhat less strongly, are innovative problem-solving behaviors of work group members and their estimates of how effective the work group is in fulfilling its part of the organization's mission.

Prediction 1-C receives strong confirmation by the data presented in Table 6 and Figure 10. Reactions of individuals to their membership in the organization are strongly related to the degree of goal integration they experience. The strongest relationship in this set is with the individual motivation index. Our goal integration measures explain 25 per cent of the variance

Table 4

RELATIONSHIP OF GOAL INTEGRATION TO
DEPARTMENT FUNCTIONING

N = 18 Departments

Measures of Department Functioning	Predictor Variables					
	Goal Integration Index #1		Goal Integration Index #2		R	R^2
	η	β	η	β		
Communication	.60*	.53	.41	.33	.51	.26
Coordination	.60*	.48	.48	.30	.49	.24
Total Influence	.73**	.70	.38	.21	.66*	.43*
Influence Distribution	.17	.10	.16	.11	.001	.001

[1]The correction for degrees of freedom was too large to permit meaningful calculation of this R or R^2. They should be interpreted as being zero.
*p <.05
**p <.01

Figure 8

RELATIONSHIP OF GOAL INTEGRATION TO
DEPARTMENT FUNCTIONING

N = 18 Departments

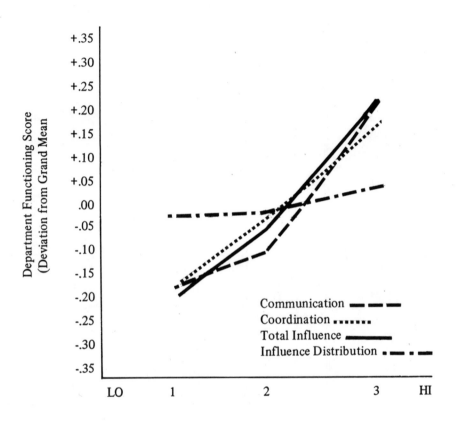

Goal Integration Category

Table 5

RELATIONSHIP OF GOAL INTEGRATION TO
WORK GROUP FUNCTIONING

N = 233 Work Groups

Measures of Work Group Functioning	Predictor Variables					
	Goal Integration Index #1		Goal Integration Index #2		R	R^2
	η	β	η	β		
Interaction	.24*	.17	.28**	.23	.27**	.07**
Coordination	.27**	.22	.29**	.24	.31**	.10**
Innovation	.15	.09	.26**	.24	.21*	.04*
Effectiveness	.21*	.17	.20	.15	.18*	.03*

*p < .05
**p < .01

Figure 9

RELATIONSHIP OF GOAL INTEGRATION TO WORK GROUP FUNCTIONING

N = 233 Work Groups

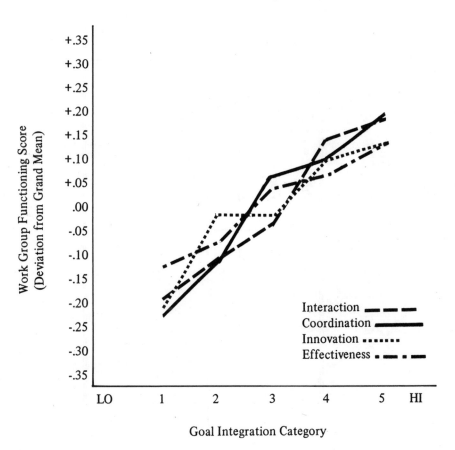

Goal Integration Category

Table 6

RELATIONSHIP OF GOAL INTEGRATION TO
INDIVIDUAL MEMBER REACTIONS

N = 1,781 Individuals

Measures of Individual Member Reactions	Predictor Variables					
	Goal Integration Index #1		Goal Integration Index #2		R	R^2
	η	β	η	β		
Motivation	.44**	.41	.29**	.26	.50**	.25**
Satisfaction	.42**	.41	.22**	.19	.45**	.20**
Commitment	.31**	.30	.26**	.25	.39**	.15**
Health Reactions	.08	.09	.08*	.08	.08*	.01*

*p <.05
**p <.01

Figure 10

RELATIONSHIP OF GOAL INTEGRATION TO INDIVIDUAL MEMBER REACTIONS

N = 1,781 Individuals

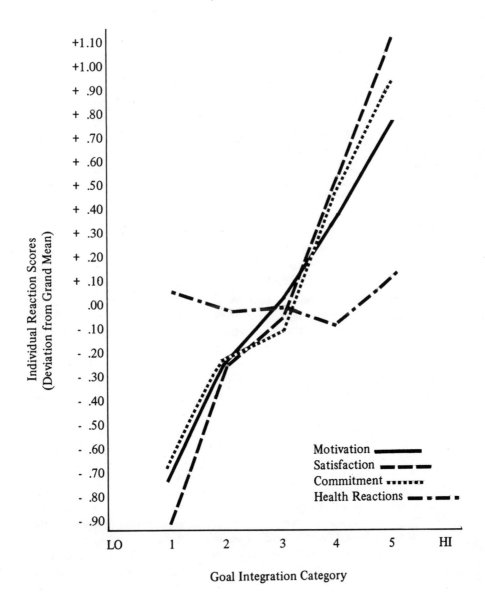

Goal Integration Category

in this motivation index. Also strongly related is our measure of individual satisfaction, combining satisfaction with the job and with the organization as a whole. Twenty per cent of the variance in this satisfaction index is explained by our goal integration measures. Individuals' feelings of loyalty and commitment to the organization are also substantially related to the amount of goal integration they experience. The only measure of individual reactions that failed to show any notable relationship to goal integration was the health reactions index—an attempt to measure work-related nervousness and tension. This lack of relationship might suggest either that nervousness and tension are not related to goal integration or that the health reactions index is not an adequate measure of these phenomena. Experience with this measure in other organization studies leads us to suspect that the trouble lies with the measure itself. The health reactions index has consistently provided highly skewed distributions and has consistently failed to show notable relationships to measures of other organizational behaviors.

The overall results presented in this section seem to provide a reasonable confirmation of general hypothesis 1 and justify the conclusion that the degree of goal integration present is significantly related to the quality of an organization's functioning and the reactions of individuals to their membership in the organization. The concept of goal integration appears to have sufficient explanatory power regarding these phenomena to justify the search for processes which produce high levels of goal integration.

Goal Integration Mechanisms and Level of Goal Integration Achieved

In this section we will present results related to general hypothesis 2, which asserts that the use of goal integration mechanisms associated with the exchange, socialization and accommodation models significantly affects the degree of goal integration achieved in an organization. As mentioned in Chapter 2, we use data at the work group level in these analyses because the concept of goal integration mechanisms refers to processes which characterize organizational units, and work groups provide the most adequate sample we have of such organizational units.

Data in Table 7 and Figure 11 concern the use of exchange mechanisms and their relation to the level of goal integration achieved. As can be readily seen from these data, prediction 2-A is definitely not confirmed—there is no evidence to support a conclusion that the use of exchange mechanisms is positively related to the degree of goal integration achieved in an organization. With regard to the use of pay as an exchange mechanism, exactly the opposite conclusion is suggested—the more pay is used as an exchange mechanism, the lower is the achieved level of goal integration. Results regarding the use of informal social relations as an exchange mechanism are less consistent than those for pay, but equally disconfirming for prediction 2-A. Our measure of

Table 7

USE OF EXCHANGE MECHANISMS AND
EXTENT OF GOAL INTEGRATION ACHIEVED

N = 233 Work Groups

Goal Integration Measures	Predictor Variables: Exchange Mechanisms					
	Pay		Informal Social Relations		R	R^2
	η	β	η	β		
Index #1	(.24)[1]**	(.24)	(.12)|	(.12)	(.19)*	.04*
Index #2	(.06)	(.05)	.19	.19	.08	.01
Summary Index	(.18)	(.18)	.19	.19	(.19)*	.03*

[1]Parentheses indicate a negative relationship
*p <.05
**p <.01

Figure 11

USE OF EXCHANGE MECHANISMS AND
EXTENT OF GOAL INTEGRATION ACHIEVED

N = 233 Work Groups

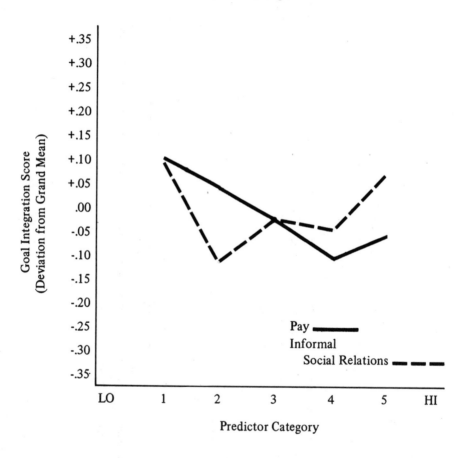

informal social relations relates negatively to the first goal integration index, and positively to the second index. It shows a curvilinear relationship to the summary goal integration index. Pay and informal social relations, taken together, explain only 3 per cent of the variance in our summary measure of goal integration.

Socialization mechanisms show considerably stronger relationships to goal integration than do exchange mechanisms, as can be seen in Table 8 and Figure 12. Leader socialization shows a somewhat stronger relation to goal integration than does peer socialization, but both relationships are positive and significant. Together, these two socialization mechanisms explain 11 per cent of the variance in our summary goal integration measure. Prediction 2-B thus appears to be confirmed—measures of the use of socialization mechanisms within organizational units do show significant positive relationships to measures of the degree of goal integration present in these units.

Results regarding the use of accommodation mechanisms appear in Table 9 and Figure 13. These data strongly confirm prediction 2-C, which asserts that measures of the use of accommodation mechanisms will show significant positive relationships to measures of goal integration. Role design and participation show equally strong relationships to goal integration, and measures of the use of these two mechanisms, taken together, explain 30 per cent of the variance in our summary goal integration index.

Overall, the results presented in this section provide a partial confirmation of general hypothesis 2. The use of goal integration mechanisms associated with the *socialization* and *accommodation* models do significantly affect the degree of goal integration achieved in an organizational unit. The use of mechanisms associated with the *exchange* model, however, show inconsistent, generally low, and sometimes negative relationships to the level of goal integration achieved.

The data presented in this section are also relevant to general hypothesis 3 and prediction 3-A, which posit differential effectiveness of the three models in ability to produce high levels of goal integration. As can be seen in Tables 7, 8 and 9, the multiple correlation coefficients relating exchange, socialization and accommodation mechanisms to the summary goal integration index are -.19, .32 and .55, respectively. These figures confirm prediction 3-A. Measures of the use of accommodation mechanisms do show higher positive relationships to goal integration than is true for measures of the use of socialization mechanisms. Socialization mechanisms, in turn, are more highly related to goal integration measures than are exchange mechanisms.

Except for the failure of exchange mechanisms to show significant positive relationships to goal integration, then, the major hypotheses and predictions of this study were generally confirmed. Goal integration is significantly related to the quality of functioning of departmental and work group

Table 8

USE OF SOCIALIZATION MECHANISMS AND
EXTENT OF GOAL INTEGRATION ACHIEVED

N = 233 Work Groups

Goal Integration Measures	Predictor Variables: Socialization Mechanisms					
	Leader Socialization		Peer Socialization			
	η	β	η	β	R	R^2
Index #1	.32**	.31	.21*	.12	.29**	.08**
Index #2	.27**	.22	.20*	.12	.23*	.05*
Summary Index	.35**	.31	.25**	.12	.32**	.11**

*p <.05
**p <.01

Figure 12

USE OF SOCIALIZATION MECHANISMS AND
EXTENT OF GOAL INTEGRATION ACHIEVED

N = 233 Work Groups

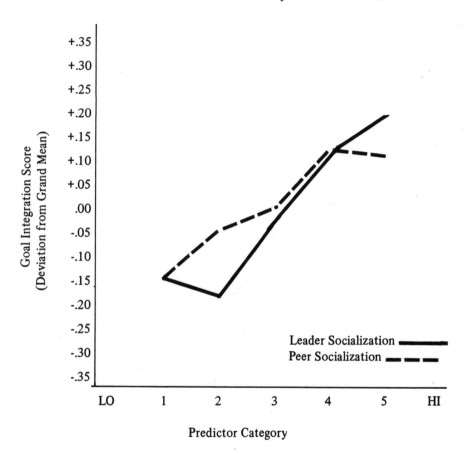

Predictor Category

Table 9

USE OF ACCOMMODATION MECHANISMS AND
EXTENT OF GOAL INTEGRATION ACHIEVED

N = 233 Work Groups

Goal Integration Measures	Predictor Variables: Accommodation Mechanisms					
	Role Design		Participation		R	R^2
	η	β	η	β		
Index #1	.50**	.32	.51**	.33	.55**	.30**
Index #2	.34**	.27	.29**	.21	.35**	.12**
Summary Index	.50**	.31	.50**	.35	.55**	.30**

**p $<$.01

Figure 13

USE OF ACCOMMODATION MECHANISMS AND
EXTENT OF GOAL INTEGRATION ACHIEVED

N = 233 Work Groups

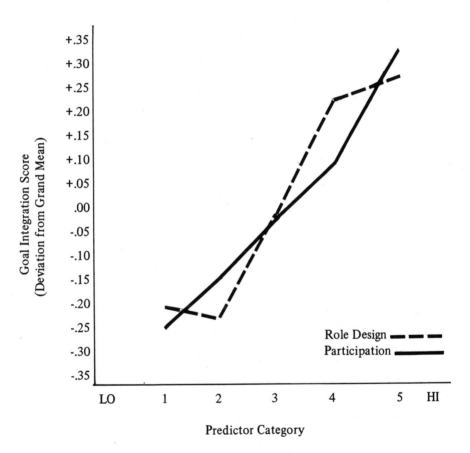

Predictor Category

units. It also relates strongly to the reactions of individuals to the organization. The use of socialization and accommodation mechanisms is significantly related to the degree of goal integration achieved in an organizational unit. Finally, the three models differ in the strength of their relationships to goal integration, the accommodation model showing the strongest relationships, with the socialization model in second place and the exchange model showing low and sometimes negative relationships to goal integration.

The Conditioning Effects of Demographic Variables

General question 2 from Chapter 2 asks whether the relationship between the use of particular goal integration models by an organizational unit and the degree of goal integration achieved is affected by the general demographic characteristics of the unit's members or by the location of the unit in the social structure of the organization. Data related to this question is presented in Table 10. In this table, the relationship between the use of a model and the level of goal integration achieved is presented separately for different categories on five control variables.[2]

Our focus here is still on processes that characterize organizational units, and we use data from work groups to provide measures from a sample of such units.

Categories for each of the first three demographic variables in Table 10 were formed by separating the 233 work groups into two sets, roughly equal in size, on the basis of the distribution of group mean scores on demographic items in the questionnaire. The questions used for forming these categories are presented below:

Demographic Variable	*Questionnaire Item*
Background	While you were growing up—say until you were eighteen—what kind of community did you live in for the most part?
	(1) Rural area or farm
	(2) Town or small city
	(3) Suburban area near large city
	(4) Large city
Education	How much schooling have you had?
	(1) Some grade school
	(2) Completed grade school

---

[2] Age was not included in this table, because of its high correlation with tenure ($r = .85$ across 233 work groups).

(3) Some high school
(4) Completed high school
(5) Some college
(6) Completed college

Tenure   When did you first come to work here?

(1) Less than 1 year ago
(2) Between 1 and 5 years ago
(3) Between 5 and 10 years ago
(4) Between 10 and 15 years ago
(5) Between 15 and 25 years ago
(6) More than 25 years ago

Ranges of group mean scores on the above questionnaire items used to define the categories appearing in Table 10 are presented below:

Demographic Variable	*Ranges of Group Mean Scores Used to Define Categories*
Background	Rural: 1.00 to 1.94
	Urban: 1.95 to 4.00
Education	High school or less: 1.00 to 4.32
	Some college: 4.33 to 6.00
Tenure	0-19 Years: 1.00 to 5.31
	20+ Years: 5.32 to 6.00

Categories for the last two demographic variables appearing in Table 10 were formed by using codes assigned to work groups by the researcher to indicate their hierarchical level or functional specialty. Groups in the non-management category consist of persons who have no formal supervisory responsibilities and who are located at the bottom of the organization, as defined by organization charts. Management groups consist of persons who have supervisory responsibilities or whose work, even though not supervisory in nature, places them above production or clerical workers in overall status. The latter consist mostly of professional employees or persons in staff positions. With regard to functional specialty, the production category includes work groups from the Processing and Maintenance Divisions of the refinery, while the research and development and administration category consists of groups from the Administrative Division, which includes both staff and technical research departments.

A number of interesting observations can be made concerning the data presented in Table 10. First, it provides additional confirmation of general hypothesis 3 concerning the differential effectiveness of the three models in producing high levels of goal integration. Within every column of Table 10 the

Table 10

USE OF GOAL INTEGRATION MODELS AND
EXTENT OF GOAL INTEGRATION ACHIEVED
CONTROLLING ON DEMOGRAPHIC VARIABLES
(Kendall's Tau—Work Group Data)

Goal Integration Models	Background		Education		Tenure		Level		Function	
	Rural N=116	Urban N=117	High school or less N=118	Some College N=115	0-19 years N=109	20+ years N=124	Non-mgmt. N=116	Mgmt. N=117	Production N=162	R & D Admin. N=71
Exchange	.09 **	-.14	.24 **	-.21	-.18 **	.03	.20 **	-.08	.13 **	-.35
Socialization	.42 **	.12	.38 *	.16	.18	.29	.23	.23	.25	.23
Accommodation	.48	.40	.46	.42	.43	.48	.33	.36	.38 **	.59

*Difference significant at .05 level of confidence
**Difference significant at .01 level of confidence
NOTE: See Appendix C for the procedure used in testing the significance of differences between taus.

order of the relationships is the same—the accommodation model always shows the strongest relationship to goal integration, followed in turn by the socialization and exchange models.

A second general observation is that the three models differ not only in *level* of effectiveness but also in the *generality* of their effectiveness across organizational units which differ in terms of the five demographic variables listed. It is especially interesting to note that the three models fall in the same order regarding the generality of their effectiveness as they do regarding the overall level of their effectiveness. Average differences among the five pairs of taus presented for each model in Table 10 are .09 for the accommodation model, .15 for the socialization model and .33 for the exchange model.

The accommodation model, it appears, is not only the most effective of the three models in terms of its ability to generate high levels of goal integration. It is also the most general of the three models, showing approximately equal effectiveness when applied to work groups which differ in terms of their members' rural/urban backgrounds, average education and length of service, and management or non-management status. The only notable variation in effectiveness of the accommodation model is related to the general type of work performed by the group. This model is more effective with research and development or administrative groups (tau = .59) than with groups performing production work (tau = .38). This difference pales somewhat in importance, however, when it is noted that the lower of these two taus is larger than all but one of the taus associated with the exchange or socialization models in Table 10.

The socialization model, not quite so effective as the accommodation model in overall ability to generate high levels of goal integration, is also somewhat less consistent in effectiveness when applied to work groups which differ on the demographic variables presented in Table 10. Unlike the accommodation model, socialization works equally well with production as with administrative or research and development groups. It is also equally effective with non-management as with managerial work groups. The socialization model works somewhat better with groups of lower average education than with groups composed mostly of persons with some exposure to college, and is slightly more effective with long-service groups than with those of shorter average tenure. The greatest variation in effectiveness of this model is related to the rural/urban backgrounds of most group members. The socialization model works considerably better in groups composed mostly of persons with rural backgrounds (tau = .42) than in groups whose members are of predominately urban background (tau = .12). This finding confirms the speculative hypothesis offered in Chapter 2 that persons of rural background, being less alienated from middle-class norms valuing hard work and loyalty to employer, would be more likely than their urban counterparts to rally around organization objectives in response to the persuasive efforts of leaders and peers.

According to the data appearing in Table 10, the exchange model is not only the least effective in generating high levels of goal integration, it is also the least stable of the three models, showing wide variations in effectiveness when applied to work groups which differ in their standing on the five demographic variables being considered here. On each of these five variables, a change in the kind of work groups to which the exchange model is applied results in a significant change from a zero or positive relationship to a negative relationship between use of this model and level of goal integration achieved. The largest difference in effectiveness is associated with differences in functional specialty. While use of the exchange model shows a low positive relationship to goal integration when applied to production groups (tau = .13), the relationship changes to a substantially negative one for research and development or administrative groups (tau = -.35). A difference of similar magnitude occurs with regard to work groups differing in the average education of members. The exchange model shows some ability to generate goal integration in work groups whose average education level is high school or less (tau = .24). It has an equally *negative* effect, however, in work groups consisting primarily of college-trained members (tau = -.21). The location of a work group in the hierarchical structure also affects the ability of the exchange model to generate goal integration. Use of this model shows a moderately low positive relation to goal integration in work groups composed of non-managerial personnel (tau = .20). This relationship becomes slightly negative for groups composed of supervisory and managerial personnel (tau = -.08). Somewhat smaller variations in effectiveness of the exchange model are associated with average tenure and rural/urban background of group members. Its use is negatively related to goal integration in groups whose average tenure is less than about 20 years (tau = -.18), but shows essentially no relationship for groups whose members average about 20 or more years of service (tau = .03). Similarly, use of the exchange model in groups of predominately urban background *lowers* the level of goal integration (tau = -.14), but has essentially no effect in groups of predominately rural background (tau = .09). Thus, the effectiveness of the exchange model appears to be limited to groups of generally lower social or organizational status, namely groups of lower educational levels and non-managerial status. It is definitely counter-effective in the generally higher-status groups composed of college-trained members and those performing research or administrative functions.

Question 2-A from Chapter 2, then, must be answered separately for each of the three goal integration models. Relationships between measures of the use of an *accommodation* model and measures of the degree of goal integration achieved are, in general, *not* different for organizational units which differ in their standing on a variety of demographic variables. The *socialization* model shows some differences in the strength of its relationship to goal integration measures when applied to groups differing on these variables. Finally, the *exchange* model shows numerous differences in the strength of its relationships to goal integration when it is used with groups which differ in terms of the rural/urban background of their members, the average tenure or educational level of members, or in terms of the kind of work the groups perform or their location in the hierarchical structure of the organization.

Relationships Among the Use of Different Models and Mechanisms

General question 3 asks how the various goal integration models or mechanisms relate to each other, and reflects an interest in determining whether the different models or mechanisms are used together or whether they tend to serve as substitutes for one another.

Table 11 presents data related to question 3-A, concerning relationships among summary measures of the use of the three goal integration models.

Table 11

CORRELATIONS AMONG MEASURES OF THE USE OF
EXCHANGE, SOCIALIZATION AND ACCOMMODATION MODELS
N = 233 Work Groups

	Exchange	Socialization
Socialization	.07	
Accommodation	-.20**	.46**

**p <.01

The correlations in this table indicate that the accommodation and socialization models tend to be used together to a moderate extent ($r = .46$). About 20 per cent of the variation in use of one of these models can be explained by variation in the use of the other model. The socialization and exchange models are essentially independent of one another, sometimes being used together and sometimes not ($r = .07$). Finally, the exchange and accommodation models, with a correlation of $-.20$, show a mild tendency to serve as substitutes for one another rather than being used together. Because the relationship is fairly small, the most accurate conclusion might be that these two models are largely independent of one another, sometimes being used together, somewhat more often serving as substitutes for each other.

With regard to ideas concerning consistency within management systems, which have been proposed by Rensis Likert and were summarized in Chapter 2, these data suggest that the accommodation and socialization models belong to a single management system, while the exchange model belongs to a separate system. More specifically, the accommodation and socialization models appear to belong together in a management system similar to the one Likert describes as a "participative group" system, while the exchange model seems to belong in a management system similar to the one he characterizes as "benevolent authoritative" (Likert, 1967, pp. 13-24). The theoretical compatibility of the accommodation model with the participative group system is evident from the similar emphasis placed on member participation in goal-setting, decision-making and influence processes. High acceptance and support of organizational goals at all levels in both the formal and informal organizations, which are said to characterize the participative group system of management, imply processes similar to those called for by the socialization model, namely leaders and peers verbally supporting objectives and modeling high work performance. The compatibility of the exchange model with the benevolent authoritative system is evident in the shared concern with economic motives, the use of positive and negative reward practices as a way of using motives, and the similar implication of an alienated, bargaining-type relationship between the individual and the organization. The data in Table 11 support empirically these theoretically reasonable associations.

The data in Table 11 are also consistent with the material in Chapters 1 and 2 which associates the socialization and accommodation models with theoretical positions of currently popular social-psychological organization theorists, and the exchange model more closely with classical and neoclassical organization theory, which the social psychologists at least partially reject. In other words, the social-psychological theorists cited can be characterized as proposing the use of accommodation and socialization models as *alternatives* to the exchange model, which they reject as not capturing the essence of effective management practice. The data support these theoretical associations by indicating that the two models supported by the social psychologists tend to be used with each other, while neither of these models is consistently used along with the model which these theorists reject as being based on a limited and inaccurate organization theory.

Questions 3-B, C and D concern relationships between the different mechanisms within each goal integration model. Data relevant to these questions appear in Table 12. Measures of the use of pay and the use of informal social relations as exchange mechanisms correlate .14, suggesting that organizational units which use one of these mechanisms may or may not use the other concurrently. These mechanisms are relatively independent of each other conceptually and in practice, although they both embody the basic assumptions of the exchange model.

Measures of leader socialization and peer socialization correlate .51, indicating a moderately strong tendency for these two processes to be used concurrently in organizational units. This finding is not surprising given the similarity in content of the questionnaire items used to measure these two processes—the behaviors involved are identical; the only difference concerns whether the behaviors are exhibited by the respondent's superior or by his peers. This result is also consistent with the findings of leadership research which suggests an 'organizational climate' effect whereby the leadership behavior of persons at a given level in an organization tends to mirror the behavior of their immediate superiors (Bowers and Seashore, 1966; Fleishman, 1953). The present data indicate that about 25 per cent of the variation in peer socialization can be explained by variation in the parallel behavior of the immediate superior.

Table 12

CORRELATIONS BETWEEN MEASURES OF THE USE OF DIFFERENT MECHANISMS WITHIN EACH GOAL INTEGRATION MODEL

N = 233 Work Groups

Goal Integration Mechanisms

Exchange Mechanisms:	
Pay with Informal Social Relations	.14**
Socialization Mechanisms:	
Leader Socialization with Peer Socialization	.51**
Accommodation Mechanisms:	
Role Design with Participation	.60**

**p $<$.01

Measures of the use of role design and the use of participation as accommodation mechanisms correlate .60, indicating that concurrent use of these two mechanisms occurs fairly frequently in organizational units. These two processes are conceptually distinct, as is true of the two exchange mechanisms. But unlike the two exchange mechanisms, role design and participation tend to be used together in practice.

The data in Tables 11 and 12, then, suggest the following answer to general question 3: The accommodation and socialization models tend to be used together in practice, while each of these is relatively independent of the use of the exchange model. Within the exchange model, pay and informal social relations tend to be used independently of one another, although there is no evidence that the use of one precludes use of the other. Leader and peer socialization show a moderately strong tendency to be used concurrently and not as substitutes for each other. Within the accommodation model, the use of role design and the use of participation show a strong relationship, implying that these two processes are often used together.

The Effect of Using Multiple Approaches to Achieving Goal Integration

Data presented in Tables 13 and 14 are related to general question 4 concerning the effect on goal integration of using multiple versus single goal integration models or mechanisms. In Table 13, the zero-order eta coefficients, relating summary measures of the use of *each* goal integration model to measures of goal integration, are compared to the unadjusted multiple correlation coefficient which relates goal integration scores simultaneously to measures of the use of the three models. To maintain comparability with the zero-order correlations, the multiple R has not been adjusted for degrees of freedom. These data suggest a generally negative answer to question 4-A — measures of the use of the three models do *not* show a higher positive relationship to goal integration scores when taken all together than does any one taken by itself. The multiple correlation coefficients relating the three use-of-model scores to the three goal integration indices are only slightly higher than the highest of the zero-order coefficients. In general, it is about as easy to predict the amount of goal integration present in an organizational unit from knowledge about only the extent to which the accommodation model is used as it is from knowledge of the extent of use of all three models.

Question 4-B also receives a generally negative answer from data presented in Table 14. For the exchange model, the informal social relations measure taken alone shows higher positive (or lower negative) relationships to goal integration than do measures of both pay and informal social relations taken together. Within the socialization model, leader socialization by itself exhibits relationships to goal integration that are very nearly as high as the relationships generated by leader and peer socialization taken together. For the accommodation model, either role design or participation measures taken singly can predict goal integration about as well as measures of the two mechanisms taken together.

These generally negative results have little meaning with regard to the exchange model, because it has already been shown to be generally ineffective in generating high levels of goal integration. Implications of these data for the socialization and accommodation models, however, are of some interest. There are two conditions which are especially likely to produce high multiple-correlation coefficients relative to the zero-order correlations of individual predictors. One of these is a situation in which each predictor is highly related to the dependent variable but is essentially unrelated to the other predictors. A second condition involves predictors which are highly related to each other

Table 13

COMPARISON OF SINGLE AND
MULTIPLE RELATIONSHIPS BETWEEN
USE OF GOAL INTEGRATION MODELS
AND EXTENT OF GOAL INTEGRATION ACHIEVED

N = 233 Work Groups

Goal Integration Measures	Zero-Order Relationships (eta)			Multiple R (unadjusted)
	Exchange Model	Socialization Model	Accommodation Model	
Index #1	(.20)[1]	.31**	.58**	.61**
Index #2	.17	.30**	.32**	.43**
Summary Index	.21*	.35**	.56**	.61**

[1]Parentheses indicate a negative relationship

*p < .05
**p < .01

Table 14

COMPARISON OF SINGLE AND MULTIPLE RELATIONSHIPS BETWEEN USE OF GOAL INTEGRATION MECHANISMS AND EXTENT OF GOAL INTEGRATION ACHIEVED

N =   233 Work groups

Goal Integration	Zero-order Relations (eta)		Multiple R (unadjusted)
Exchange Mechanisms	Pay	Informal Social Relations	
Index #1	(.24)**	.12	(.27)*
Index #2	(.06)	.19	.20
Summary Index	(.18)	.19	(.26)*
Socialization Mechanisms	Leader	Peer	
Index #1	.32**	.21*	.34**
Index #2	.27**	.20*	.29*
Summary Index	.35**	.25**	.37**
Accommodation Mechanisms	Role Design	Participation	
Index #1	.50**	.51**	.57**
Index #2	.34**	.29**	.39**
Summary Index	.50**	.50**	.57**

[1]Parentheses indicate a negative relationship
 *p. <.05
**p. <.01

but which show quite different relationships to the dependent variable. Our data do not match either of these conditions. What we have, rather, is a situation in which the predictors are fairly highly related to each other and show similar relationships to the dependent variable. For example, we saw earlier that measures of the use of a socialization model and measures of the use of an accommodation model correlated .46. In Table 13 we see that each model has a moderate to strong positive relationship to the dependent variable, goal integration. Such a situation is not likely to produce a high multiple correlation coefficient between the two predictors taken together and the dependent variable. What appears to be happening here is that the socialization and accommodation models are explaining overlapping portions of the variance in goal integration.

Conditions similar to those just described also hold for the different goal integration mechanisms within the socialization and accommodation models. The use of leader and peer socialization correlate .51, as we noted earlier, and each shows a moderate positive relationship to goal integration in Table 14. Similarly, the use of role design and participation correlate .60 and each of these mechanisms shows a fairly high positive relationship to goal integration. Within each of these two models, then, the different mechanisms appear to be explaining overlapping portions of the variation in goal integration.

The implications of these results for our theoretical model are not entirely clear. On one hand, they seem to imply that we have not been able to isolate and measure goal integration mechanisms that are independent of each other in terms of their ability to explain the degree of goal integration achieved in organizational units. If we could isolate mechanisms which tended not to be highly related in use and each of which was highly related to goal integration, then we could more accurately predict the level of goal integration to be expected from joint use of the mechanisms. If Likert's ideas regarding consistency in management systems have any truth, however, it is unrealistic to expect that such mechanisms will be found. All mechanisms consistent with a given goal integration model will tend to be related in practice. Similarly, different goal integration models which are consistent with a given management system will tend to be used together in practice. These two derivations from the consistency proposition appear to hold true in our data concerning the use of the socialization and accommodation models, and the specific mechanisms within each of these models.

The most reasonable conclusions to be drawn from these data regarding our theoretical model might be the following. Assuming that the model represents a causal framework, these data indicate that goal integration is multiply-caused. The various causal conditions are correlated in practice and overlap or duplicate each other in their effects on the level of goal integration achieved. Specifically, the data of this study suggest that goal integration is caused by the use of socialization and accommodation mechanisms. These mechanisms tend to be used together in practice and have similar, non-unique effects on the level of goal integration achieved.

"Positive" Versus "Negative" Approaches to Achieving Goal Integration

General question 5 from Chapter 2 asks whether it is possible to differentiate "positive" and "negative" mechanisms and whether these differ in the strength of their relationships to goal integration. For each goal integration model, one item was selected which was judged to represent a positive mechanism and one item was chosen to represent a negative mechanism. These six questionnaire items are presented below:

	Positive Mechanisms	*Negative Mechanisms*
Exchange Model	When your supervisor shows an interest in your off-the-job activities, to what extent does he do this as a way of rewarding you for getting the work out?	To what extent are informal conversations on the job permitted only when persons are performing their jobs well?
Socialization Model	Since you came to work here, to what extent have contacts with your supervisor and fellow employees increased your interest in the task activities that make up your job?	Since you came to work here, to what extent have contacts with your supervisor and fellow employees reduced your interest in activities that are not part of your work tasks?
Accommodation Model	In this company, to what extent are the interests and needs of employees taken into account when jobs are designed or work activities are assigned?	To what extent is this company willing to change or give up work methods or objectives which go against the needs and interests of employees?

For the exchange model, the two items represent the difference between offering a social incentive as a *reward* for contributing to organizational objectives and withholding a social incentive as *punishment* for failure to contribute. With regard to the socialization model, the two items concern the difference between inducing an individual to *adopt* some new personal goals that are in line with organizational objectives and trying to get him to *give up* some of his existing goals that might detract from his contribution to organization objectives. For the accommodation model, the distinction represented by the two items is between the organization's *adopting* objectives or work methods that are congruent with individual goals and *abandoning* objectives or methods that conflict with individual goals. The differences represented by these item pairs bear some resemblance to distinctions that have been drawn between "compromise" and "integrative" solutions that may result from organizational decision-making or problem-solving processes (Metcalf and Urwick, 1942; Maier and Hoffman, 1961). In compromise solutions, one or both parties lose or give up something whereas in integrative solutions a win-lose definition of the problem is avoided and ways are found to satisfy the needs of both parties.

Table 15 and Figure 14 indicate the relationships between use of the three positive mechanisms and level of goal integration achieved. As can be seen from these data, the relationships are fairly high and positive for the socialization and accommodation items, and positive but somewhat lower for the exchange item. Taken together, these three positive mechanism measures explain 33 per cent of the variance in our summary goal integration measure—a rather impressive result.

Results related to the three negative mechanisms are presented in Table 16 and Figure 15. These data reveal a predominately negative relationship between the socialization item and goal integration. The relationship for the exchange item is moderately low and curvilinear. The "negative" accommodation item, however, shows a moderately high positive relationship to goal integration. This negative accommodation mechanism is the only one of the three that can be said to have a positive effect on the level of goal integration. The different results generated by negative accommodation on one hand and negative exchange and socialization on the other hand can probably be explained by the assumption that sacrifice on the part of the organization is less likely to be seen by employees as damaging to goal integration than are sacrifices they have to make themselves. The multiple correlation coefficient is somewhat difficult to interpret in this case because of the curvilinear relationship revealed for the exchange item and the negative relationship of the socialization item to goal integration. While a multiple correlation of .45 is substantial, in this instance it cannot be interpreted as indicating the extent to which these three items together show a positive linear relationship to goal integration.

Comparing the data in Tables 15 and 16 provides a positive answer to question 5-A. Measures of the use of "positive" mechanisms from the three goal integration models do show higher positive relationships to measures of

Table 15

USE OF POSITIVE MECHANISMS AND
EXTENT OF GOAL INTEGRATION ACHIEVED

N = 233 Work Groups

Goal Integration Measures	Predictor Variables: Positive Mechanisms									
	Positive Exchange		Positive Socialization		Positive Accommodation					
	η	β	η	β	η	β	R	R^2
Index #1	.14	.08	.53**	.36	.53**	.38	.60**	.36**
Index #2	.17	.15	.26**	.16	.29**	.21	.28**	.08**
Summary Index	.16	.11	.51**	.34	.51**	.35	.57**	.33**

**p < .01

Figure 14

USE OF POSITIVE MECHANISMS AND
EXTENT OF GOAL INTEGRATION ACHIEVED

N = 233 Work Groups

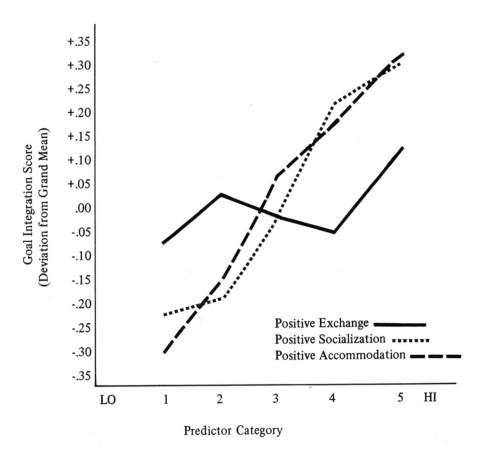

Predictor Category

Table 16

USE OF NEGATIVE MECHANISMS AND
EXTENT OF GOAL INTEGRATION ACHIEVED

N = 233 Work Groups

| | Predictor Variables: Negative Mechanisms | | | | | | | |
Goal Integration Measures	Negative Exchange		Negative Socialization		Negative Accommodation		R	R^2
	η	β	η	β	η	β		
Index #1	.22*	.12	(.30)1**	(.25)	.43**	.39	.47**	.22**
Index #2	.21*	:19	.10	.09	.26**	.25	.25**	.06**
Summary Index	.25**	.16	(.24)**	(.19)	.42**	.38	.45**	.20**

1Parentheses indicate a negative relationship
*p <.05
**p <.01

Figure 15

USE OF NEGATIVE MECHANISMS AND
EXTENT OF GOAL INTEGRATION ACHIEVED

N = 233 Work Groups

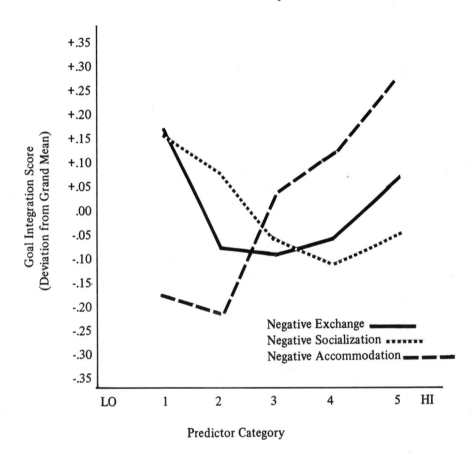

goal integration than measures of the use of "negative" mechanisms from the three models. Even though the negative accommodation item exhibits a substantial positive relationship to goal integration (eta = .42), it is lower than the one generated by the positive accommodation mechanism (eta = .51).

Individual Differences in Importance of Particular Goals

In general question 6 we are concerned with whether the ability of a particular mechanism to produce high levels of goal integration is affected by individual differences in the importance of the goal implicit in that mechanism. For example, is the effectiveness of pay as an exchange mechanism a function of how important money is to the persons to whom this mechanism is applied? For three questionnaire items representing the use of exchange mechanisms and three items representing the use of accommodation mechanisms, there were available corresponding items which could be used as measures of the importance assigned to the goals or incentives implicit in the use of these mechanisms. The items representing use of particular mechanisms and the paired items used to measure importance of the goals implicit in those mechanisms are presented below:

	Measure of the use of this mechanism	*Measure of the importance of the goal implicit in this mechanism*
Exchange Mechanisms:		
Pay	To what extent are you paid for doing things which are not in themselves interesting to you?	How important is it to you to have a job which pays a high salary or wages?
Personal Interest From Superior	When your supervisor shows an interest in your off-the-job activities, to what extent does he do this as a way of rewarding you for getting the work out?	To what extent is your supervisor willing to listen to your problems? Ideal: This is how I'd *like* it to be.

| Informal Peer Relations | To what extent are informal conversations on the job permitted only when persons are performing their jobs well? | To what extent does your supervisor encourage the people who work for him to exchange opinions and ideas? Ideal: This is how I'd *like* it to be. |

Accommodation Mechanisms:

| Job Uses Abilities | To what extent does your job give you a chance to use your best abilities—to do the things you are best at? | How important is it to you to have a job which makes use of your best abilities— which allows you to do the things you are best at? |

| Job Activities Interesting | To what extent do you enjoy performing the actual day-to-day activities that make up your job? | How important is it to you to have day-to-day work activities that are interesting and enjoyable to perform? |

| Frequency of Group Meetings | How often does your supervisor hold group meetings where he and the people who work for him can really discuss things together? Actual: This is how it is *now*. | How often does your supervisor hold group meetings where he and the people who work for him can really discuss things together? Ideal: This is how I'd *like* it to be. |

Answer alternatives for the last question above, concerning the frequency of group meetings, range from "never" to "more often than once per month." Each question in the above list which is followed by the words "Ideal: This is how I'd *like* it to be," is the second part of a two-part question which asks the respondent, first, how things are now and, secondly, how he would like them to be. Each of the questions in the right-hand part of the above list was used as the basis for dividing the 1,781 respondents into sub-sets differing in terms of whether they assign high, medium or low importance to a particular goal or incentive. The goal or incentive involved is the same one implicit in the use of the mechanisms described by the paired items in the left-hand part

Table 17

USE OF GOAL INTEGRATION MECHANISMS AND
EXTENT OF GOAL INTEGRATION ACHIEVED
CONTROLLING ON IMPORTANCE OF GOAL
(Kendall's Tau—Individual Data)

Importance of Goal	Exchange Mechanisms						Accommodation Mechanisms					
	Pay		Personal Interest From Superior		Informal Peer Relations		Job Uses Abilities		Job Activities Interesting		Frequency Of Group Meetings	
	N	Tau	N	Tau	N	Tau	N	Tau	N	Tau	N	Tau
High	565	-.04	759	.12[1]	595	.06	609	.362	511	.402	469	.25
Medium	739	-.15[3]	592	.08	665	-.023	678	.29[3]	722	.303	652	.22
Low	285	.004	152	.06	264	.074	285	.24	366	.27	402	.22

[1]Difference between high and low groups significant at .05 level of confidence
[2]Difference between high and low groups significant at .01 level of confidence
[3]Difference between high and medium groups significant at .01 level of confidence
[4]Difference between medium and low groups significant at .01 level of confidence
Note: See Appendix C for the procedure used in testing the significance of differences between taus.

of the list. Then, within each of these subsets of respondents, Kendall's tau was computed as a measure of the strength of relationship between use of the particular mechanism and our summary measure of the degree of goal integration reported by individuals. Data at the individual level were used in this analysis because our interest is focused on individual differences in goal importance, and the most precise information available about such differences exists in the questionnaire responses of individual subjects.

Results of the analysis described above appear in Table 17. With regard to the three exchange mechanism measures, the data show no consistent pattern in the strength of the relationship between use of the mechanism and level of goal integration achieved, moving from respondents who assign low importance to the goals to respondents who assign great importance to them. There is a slight indication that the use of personal interest from superiors as an exchange mechanism may be more effective with persons who assign high importance to personal interest from superiors than among persons who assign lesser importance to this goal. In general, however, the results for the exchange mechanisms are so low and inconsistent as to permit no conclusive interpretation. Data with regard to the three accommodation mechanism measures show a more consistent pattern, although the differences still are not great. Relationships between measures of two of these accommodation mechanisms and the summary measure of goal integration are significantly stronger for persons who assign high importance to the goals involved than they are for persons who assign only moderate or low importance to these goals. The greater the importance an individual attaches to having a job which is intrinsically interesting and challenging, the stronger is the relationship between the organization's provision of these conditions and the individual's experience of goal integration.

The answer to question 6-A, then, is different for the two sets of mechanisms. Measures of the use of *exchange* mechanisms do *not* show higher positive relationships to goal integration for persons who assign great importance to the goals implicit in these mechanisms than they do for persons who ascribe lesser importance to these goals. Measures of the use of *accommodation* mechanisms do show somewhat higher positive relationships to goal integration for persons who assign great importance to the goals implicit in these mechanisms than they do for persons who consider these goals to be of lesser importance.

The low and inconsistent results for the exchange mechanisms are not surprising for several reasons. First, the general inability of the exchange model to produce high levels of goal integration, revealed by results reported earlier in this chapter, would lead us to expect generally low and inconsistent relationships here as well. Secondly, except for the pay measure, the importance-of-goal measures were not closely matched to the use-of-mechanism measures. Measures designed for other purposes were adapted for use in this situation; measures designed especially to tap the importance of these particular goals to individuals would have been more appropriate but were not available. Two additional factors may be related to these inconclusive results and are also relevant when considering the generally small differences among taus that were revealed for the three accommodation mechanisms. First, there is a restricted range of scores on all the importance-of-goal measures due to a negative skewness of their response distributions. With most responses concentrated at the upper end of the scale, differences between the low and high importance categories are based on rather small differences in scores on the importance measures. Low importance, as used in Table 17, is closer to moderate importance in terms of the original response scale. So the three importance-of-goal categories do not represent great differences in the importance assigned to these goals by the respondents in this study. Secondly, it must be remembered that our measure of goal integration is not the same as a measure of member satisfaction with the organization. Our goal integration measure is intended to tap the degree of *match* between the satisfaction of individual needs and the achievement of organizational objectives. Especially with regard to the accommodation mechanism measures included in Table 17, we would expect greater differences in the taus across importance-of-goal categories if the dependent variable were a measure of individual satisfaction with the organization rather than our measure of goal integration. Individual satisfaction is only half of what is required to produce high levels of goal integration, achievement of organizational objectives also being an important part of this concept. In light of these limitations, the differences in the magnitude of taus across importance categories that were revealed for the accommodation mechanisms probably have more significance than their modest size would indicate.

Conditional Versus Unconditional Use of Incentives

General question 7 from Chapter 2 asks whether the conditional provision of incentives, implicit in the exchange model, differs from the unconditional provision of incentives in strength of relationship to goal integration. Our measures of the use of exchange mechanisms are essentially measures of the conditional use of incentives. The organization provides these material or social incentives to the individual *on the condition* that the individual contributes to achieving the organization's objectives. Included in the survey questionnaire were three questions which parallel these measures of the use of exchange mechanisms, but which do not stipulate any conditions under which these material and social incentives are provided. These three items are presented below:

Measures of the Unconditional
Provision of Incentives

Pay:

How do your wages or salary earnings compare with those of persons in other companies who have jobs similar to yours?

(1) My earnings are much lower than those of similar persons in other companies
(2) My earnings are somewhat lower
(3) About the same
(4) My earnings are somewhat higher
(5) My earnings are much higher than those of similar persons in other companies

Informal Social Relations:

Personal
Interest
from
Superior

To what extent does your supervisor take an interest in your off-the-job activities and concerns?

Informal
Peer
Relations

To what extent does your supervisor approve of and permit informal conversations among the persons in your work group?

These items parallel the three items used to indicate the use of exchange mechanisms, the only difference being that the two items above dealing with informal social relations have not been combined into an index, as were the parallel items from the exchange model.

Data presented in Table 18 and Figure 16 reveal a substantial positive relationship between the three above measures of the unconditional provision of incentives and our measures of the degree of goal integration achieved in organizational units. Taken together, these three measures explain 24 per cent of the variance in our summary index of goal integration. Comparing these data to those presented in Table 7 and Figure 11 suggests a negative answer to question 7-A: Measures of the use of exchange mechanisms do *not* show higher positive relationships to measures of goal integration than do measures of the unconditional provision of the same incentives used in those exchange mechanisms. In fact, the opposite is true—exchange mechanisms show considerably *lower* relationships to goal integration than does the unconditional provision of incentives.

These data raise some interesting questions regarding where the unconditional use of incentives fits in our theoretical model. In the discussion leading to general question 7 in Chapter 2 we indicated that our formulation of the exchange model was similar to George Homans' conception of the

Table 18

UNCONDITIONAL USE OF INCENTIVES AND
EXTENT OF GOAL INTEGRATION ACHIEVED

N = 233 Work Groups

Goal Integration Measures	Predictor Variables							
	Pay		Personal Interest From Superior		Informal Peer Relations		R	R^2
	η	β	η	β	η	β		
Index #1	.45**	.39	.30**	.19	.27**	.15	.49**	.24**
Index #2	.33**	.30	.14	.10	.28**	.24	.39**	.15**
Summary Index	.41**	.34	.28**	.18	.34**	.23	.49**	.24**

**p <.01

Figure 16

UNCONDITIONAL USE OF INCENTIVES AND
EXTENT OF GOAL INTEGRATION ACHIEVED

N = 233 Work Groups

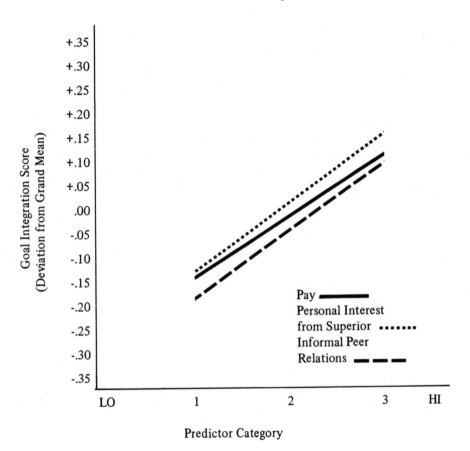

process of social exchange, both involving the offering of some valued commodity by one party *conditional upon* the receipt of another valued commodity from a second party. In contrast to this was the formulation of the social exchange process by Peter Blau who asserts that reciprocal obligations are generated when one party *unconditionally* provides some valued commodity to a second party. We also mentioned that Blau's formulation was not used in developing our concept of the exchange model because of the difficulty of differentiating its basic assumptions from those of our accommodation model, namely, that individual goals are accepted as given and the organization makes provisions for fulfilling them by the way it selects objectives, designs roles and organizes decision-making or problem-solving processes. This suggests that the unconditional use of incentives probably resembles our accommodation model more closely than it does the exchange model.

Comparing the data presented in Table 18 and Figure 16 with data presented earlier in this chapter lends support to this suggestion. Relationships between the unconditional use of incentives and goal integration bear little resemblance in magnitude or form to the relationships between use of exchange mechanisms and level of goal integration achieved (Table 7 and Figure 11). The resemblance is much greater, however, when Table 18 and Figure 16 are compared to those containing data regarding the use of accommodation mechanisms (Table 9 and Figure 13).

To expand this question somewhat and bring more specific data to bear upon it, it was decided to examine the relationships between measures of conditional and unconditional use of incentives on one hand and summary measures of the use of each goal integration model on the other hand. The product-moment correlation coefficients used for making these comparisons are presented in Table 19. Data in the lower half of this table provide strong support for the assertion that the unconditional use of incentives is most similar to the use of an accommodation model and least similar to the use of an exchange model. The average correlation between measures of the unconditional use of incentives and the accommodation model summary index is .39 (using Fisher's r to z transformation), compared to only .02 for the exchange model. In addition, these data indicate that the unconditional use of incentives bears an intermediate relationship to the use of a socialization model, the average correlation being .24.[3]

---

[3]The correlation between the measure of personal interest from supervisor and the socialization model index is .43, compared to a correlation of .39 with the accommodation model index. This might appear to weaken the above statement. The correlation of .43, however, is influenced primarily by the relation of the personal-interest-from-supervisor item to the leader socialization component of the socialization model index (r = .47). The relation of personal interest from supervisor to peer socialization is only .21. The personal-interest-from-supervisor item and the leader socialization measure have a common referent, namely the behavior of the immediate superior. The former item shares this common referent with only two of the six items that make up the accommodation model index. With

Data in the top half of Table 19 reveal just the opposite pattern of relationships for measures of the conditional use of incentives. These measures show the lowest relationship to the use of an accommodation model, with an average correlation of −.12. They relate at an intermediate level to the use of a socialization model (average r = .08). Their highest relationships are with the summary measure of the use of an exchange model (average r = .69), which is not surprising since these measures of conditional use of incentives are the components which make up the exchange model summary index.

We conclude from the data reviewed above that the unconditional use of incentives fits most appropriately in our theoretical framework alongside the accommodation model. Embodying the basic assumptions underlying this model, the unconditional provision of incentives also tends to occur in conjunction with the use of accommodation mechanisms to a significant extent. It also shows some tendency to occur in conjunction with the use of socialization mechanisms. Adding to these facts the earlier finding that the use of the socialization and accommodation models correlate .46, we might speculate that we have one cluster of processes, represented by socialization mechanisms, accommodation mechanisms and the unconditional provision of incentives, which tend to be used together and thus may be said to belong to a single management system. The management system they belong to is most likely one similar to those held to be most effective by current theorists in the social psychology of organizations (e.g., Argyris, 1964; Bennis, 1966; Likert, 1961; Schein, 1965). This cluster of processes stands apart from the kind of conditional use of incentives implied by the exchange model, which probably belongs to a management system held to be most effective by theorists at an earlier period in the development of organization theory (e.g., Taylor, 1923; Weber, 1947; Gulick and Urwick, 1937).

this in mind, the fact that personal interest from supervisor shows a slightly higher relation to the socialization than to the accommodation model index does not appear to weaken the general statement made above.

Table 19

RELATIONSHIP OF CONDITIONAL AND UNCONDITIONAL USE OF INCENTIVES
TO THE USE OF EXCHANGE, SOCIALIZATION AND ACCOMMODATION MODELS
(Product-Moment Correlations)

N = 233 Work Groups

	Exchange Model Summary Index	Socialization Model Summary Index	Accommodation Model Summary Index
Conditional Use of Incentives			
Pay	.71[1]	-.11	-.23**
Personal Interest from Superior	.68[1]	.13*	.04
Peer Relations	.66[1]	.22**	-.18**
Average r	.69[1]	.08*	-.12**
Unconditional Use of Incentives			
Pay	.00	.15*	.41**
Personal Interest from Superior	.18**	.43**	.39**
Peer Relations	-.16*	.14*	.36**
Average r	.02	.24**	.39**

[1]These correlations are spuriously high because each conditional-use-of-incentives measure is included in the exchange model summary index.

*p <.05
**p <.01

V
Discussion

A fair amount of discussion regarding the meaning of results presented in the preceding chapter was incorporated in that chapter, the implications of a particular analysis being discussed as the data were presented. In this chapter, we wish merely to elaborate a couple of points, indicate some limitations of the present study and make a few suggestions regarding further research on this topic.

Differential Generality of Management Theories

Results presented in the preceding chapter regarding the conditioning effect of demographic variables may shed some light on a recurring controversy between some organization theorists and some of their critics. This controversy concerns the generality of effectiveness of different organization theories as guides for management practice.

Current theorists who support normative theories of management practice most frequently labeled "participative" or "democratic" theories (cf., for example, Argyris, 1964; Katz and Kahn, 1966; Likert, 1961; McGregor, 1960) tend to express the following two views: (1) participative or democratic management practices are universally effective in producing favorable outcomes in terms of criteria which include productivity and long-term profitability of the organization, adaptiveness of the organization to a changing environment, and health and well-being of organization members; (2) earlier normative theories of management practice, most frequently labeled "classical" or "traditional" theories (e.g., Gulick and Urwick, 1937; Taylor, 1923; Weber, 1947), are universally limited in effectiveness in terms of the same kinds of criteria mentioned above. "Universally" in these two statements implies all types or categories of persons and all types or classes of organizations. This is probably a stronger statement than any of the participative management theorists listed would accept as a summary of their position, but

89

if a debate were to be staged, it does illustrate the side of the argument they would be likely to support. Some current critics of participative management theories (e.g., Strauss, 1963a, 1963b) have questioned both these views, asserting (1) that for certain types of organizations or certain categories of persons (e.g., mass production organizations or persons of lower skill or educational levels) the practices called for by classical theories *are* effective, and (2) the effectiveness of participative management practices is limited to certain types of organizations or categories of persons (e.g., research and development or educational organizations; middle-class, managerial or professional persons).

If we assume that our exchange model of goal integration is compatible with classical theories, that our accommodation model is compatible with participative theories and that the degree of goal integration achieved is related to organizational effectiveness, then we can bring some data from the present study to bear on this controversy. Specifically, findings regarding the conditioning effect of demographic variables, presented in Table 10, have some implications for this issue. They suggest that the participative theory supporters and their critics are both partly correct and partly incorrect. The data in Table 10 indicate that there are at least some categories of persons with which the exchange model is effective in producing goal integration, countering the assertion that practices called for by classical theories are universally limited in effectiveness. On the other hand, these data suggest that the accommodation model is effective in producing goal integration across many different categories of persons, countering the assertion that the effectiveness of participative management practices is limited to certain categories of persons. Rather than calling for either (a) the universal application of participative practices and universal rejection of classical methods or (b) the use, in a given situation of *either* participative *or* classical practices, our data suggest a third alternative, namely the universal application of participative management practices, *supplemented* in particular situations by the use of some practices called for by classical theories.

Use of Incentives in Participative Management Systems

Our findings regarding the relationship of unconditional use of incentives to degree of goal integration achieved (Table 18 and Figure 16) provide a starting point for some speculation about the use of incentives in participative management systems. In the preceding chapter we came to the conclusion that socialization mechanisms, accommodation mechanisms and the unconditional provision of incentives constitute a cluster of processes which have similar effects on goal integration, and tend to be used together in organizations. Thus, these processes might be considered as belonging to a single management system, a management system similar to those held to be most effective by a number of current organizational social psychologists. As noted in Chapter 1, socialization and accommodation mechanisms are explicitly proposed or supported by these theorists. This is not the case, however, with regard to the unconditional provision of incentives.

Most current organization theorists, including those we have listed as supporters of participative or democratic management systems, still view the use of incentives in organizations as a process involving the granting of rewards to members *conditional upon* the members' displaying some behavior of value to the organization (c.f. Argyris, 1964; McGregor, 1960; Katz and Kahn, 1966). It is true that these theorists suggest many changes from historically prevalent ways of using incentives, and that these changes make their views quite different from those that call for the kind of conditional provision of incentives implied by our exchange model. Argyris and Katz and Kahn suggest broadening the definition of "behaviors of value to the organization" to include maintaining the internal social system, creating new solutions to organizational problems, helping the organization adapt to its environment, and aiding the individual member's self development and education. Likert (1961) and McGregor (1960) suggest broadening the concept of the recipient of the reward to include groups, departments or even the entire organization. Several of these authors suggest broadening the concept of the source of rewards to harness the inherent power of groups to administer rewards and punishments to their members. All of these suggestions, however, are still made within the basic framework of a conditional provision of incentives.

The results of this study hint that a quite different basic view of the use of incentives may be compatible with the participative management systems proposed by these authors. Our data indicate that measures of the provision of material and social incentives to members, *unqualified* by conditional relationships of incentive provision to member performance, show sizable relationships to perceived goal integration (Table 18). In addition, the unconditional provision of incentives tends to be used along with goal integration mechanisms that make up the socialization and accommodation models (Table 19). These findings suggest that the unconditional provision of incentives is compatible with the use of socialization and accommodation models, which in turn are compatible with, or perhaps part of, the participative management systems proposed by the theorists referred to earlier in this section. Completing this chain of reasoning, then, is the suggestion that the unconditional use of incentives might be considered an integral part of the participative or democratic management systems proposed by some current organization theorists.

The speculative nature of this suggestion should be kept in mind, because our data bear only an oblique relation to this issue. We have no data to suggest that the kind of modified conditional use of incentives proposed by theorists such as Argyris, Likert, Katz and Kahn, or McGregor are not effective in terms of their relation to performance criteria or are not consistent with other practices called for by the formulations of these authors. Our data do suggest that the kind of conditional use of incentives implied by the exchange model are ineffective, using perceived goal integration as a criterion, and are inconsistent with socialization and accommodation mechanisms, using association-in-use as a criterion. This is suggestive evidence at best, but the idea that unconditional provision of incentives might be an integral part of participative management theory seemed intriguing enough to present in spite of its tenuous anchorage in the data of this study.

Having gone this far, we might speculate briefly about how the unconditional provision of incentives might be connected to participative management theories. Argyris (1964) and Likert (1961), for example, both stress the importance of motivational or psychological energy to organizational effectiveness. The motivational energies of individuals are one of the basic resources that organizations rely upon in carrying out their work. Anything which can increase the amount of psychological energy available could potentially increase organizational effectiveness. Both Argyris and Likert indicate that one important factor influencing the amount of psychological or motivational energy available is the person's self-esteem or sense of personal worth and importance. The more self-esteem a person has, or the more his sense of personal worth and importance is confirmed, the more psychological energy he has available to invest in various activities, including activities related to the goals of any organization to which he may belong. The less self-esteem a person has, the more his psychological energy is tied up in a search for experiences that will confirm his sense of personal worth, and the less energy there is available for other activities. The unconditional provision of incentives might be seen as a way of communicating to a person that he is valued by the organization, thus confirming his own sense of personal worth. It is as if the organization were saying to the individual, "You are valued as a person; your material and social needs are recognized, considered legitimate, and will be provided for simply because you have them." In addition, the unconditional provision of incentives avoids communicating to the person that he is valued only as an instrument and that he is regarded as an object to be manipulated by the organization, both of these messages producing a disconfirmation of the person's sense of personal worth. To make this point clearer, we could characterize the conditional use of incentives as communicating to the person, "You are valued as an instrument, for what you can do rather than for what you are; your material and social needs are recognized and will be used by the organization as a means of manipulating you to perform in the service of organizational goals." The perception of oneself as having only instrumental value and as being controlled by outside forces is not conducive to the maintenance of self-esteem. This line of reasoning suggests at least one possible link between the concept of unconditional provision of incentives and the concept of motivational or psychological energy, the latter concept being an integral part of some participative management theories.

Limitations of the Present Study and Suggestions for Further Research

Single point in time. All the data employed in this study were collected at a single point in time, which makes it impossible to verify the implied causal relationships among concepts in our theoretical model. The overall model, as pictured in Figure 5, implies that the use of goal integration mechanisms logically precedes or causes the degree of goal integration achieved. Goal integration, in turn, is assumed to logically precede or cause variations in organizational functioning and individual reactions. While the results of this study support the reasonableness of the overall model, it cannot be said that they confirm the particular causal relationships implied in the model. In future research on this topic, the collection of longitudinal data and the use of special analysis techniques, such as cross-lag correlations, could help solve this difficulty.

Single organization. Although the major variables employed in this study are intended to refer to organizations as units, all the data in this investigation come from a single organization. The use of work groups or other sub-units as units of observation in studying variables which are intended to characterize organizations is widespread in the history of organizational research and is a scientifically justifiable research procedure. It does, however, pose some difficulties. One problem is that if the use of different goal integration mechanisms is strongly influenced by general policies of the total organization, as we suspect it is, then collection of data from work groups within a single organization may result in an artificially restricted range of variation on the use-of-mechanism measures. Since this would make it more difficult to establish significant relationships between the use-of-mechanism measures and goal integration measures, it would result in a conservative bias in the present study. Another difficulty resulting from the use of data from a single organization concerns the generalizability of the results obtained. It certainly could not be argued that we have a representative sample of organizations or of work groups, and generalizations beyond the organization that provided the data should be made only with extreme caution. Both of the difficulties mentioned here argue for replication in future studies that, at a minimum, utilize data from more than one organization, ideally moving toward systematic sampling of organizations within some clearly defined population of organizations.

Measurement. The adequacy of measurement is not strictly comparable across our various goal integration mechanisms, and this could have had some effect on the results of this study. The number of items used to measure different concepts, for example, ranges from the single-item measure of the use of pay as an exchange mechanism, to the four-item index employed as a measure of the use of participation as an accommodation mechanism. All other mechanisms were measured by two-item indices. Differential reliabilities that might result from this variation in the number of items used could impose different limits on the magnitude of relationships that can be generated between the various use-of-mechanism measures and our goal integration measures. There is no evidence that this was a major problem in the present study since the single-item pay measure generated a higher relationship to one goal integration measure than did the two-item informal social relations index, and the two-item role design measure related as highly to goal integration as did the four-item participation index. Still, in future studies the quality of measurement would be increased by augmenting all the measures to some extent and attempting to avoid large differences in reliabilities of measures whose effects on a third variable are to be compared.

Another common problem from which the present study is not entirely free occurs when items used to measure different concepts have a common referent. In the present study, for example, each of the three separate measures assessing use of an exchange, socialization or accommodation model contains at least one item which has as its referent the respondent's immediate superior. Relationships among such measures could be spuriously high if numerous components of the different measures have common referents. Relationships among the measures cited above as examples of shared referents in the present study appear in Table 11. These data suggest that spuriously high relationships due to shared referents are not a serious problem in this study, although some specific interpretations do require that this problem be kept in mind (for example, see the footnote on page 86). This problem is almost impossible to eliminate entirely, but attempts to maintain some balance in the extent to which different measures have common referents can alleviate difficult problems in interpreting relationships among measures.

Theoretical status of "goal integration." In the general theoretical model employed in this study, we have treated the concept of goal integration as an intervening variable, referring to a state of affairs that "comes between" certain organizational practices (goal integration mechanisms) and certain outcomes (organizational functioning and individual reactions), and thus "explains" the relationship between these practices and outcomes. In a comparable way, Wilson (1968) uses a concept similar to that of goal integration as an intervening variable to explain the relationship between management styles and interpersonal relations in a prison organization. Other theorists, however, give a different theoretical status to the concept of goal integration. Katzell (1962), for instance, treats it as a conditioning or moderating variable—one which defines the *conditions under which* a particular management practice will show positive or negative relationships to outcome variables. As an example, Katzell suggests that participative management practices might be expected to lead to effective organizational functioning when goal integration is high but not when it is low. In this approach, goal integration is not seen as a state of affairs that comes between some organizational practice and some outcome. Rather, goal integration is seen as a state of affairs that exists *along with* the organizational practice and *interacts* with it to determine the outcome. Representing still another view, Vroom (1960) suggests that perceived goal integration may itself be considered an outcome variable, *resulting from* a member's overall satisfaction with the organization. We have not explored these alternative views of the theoretical role of goal integration as a concept. Such exploration might be a fruitful line of pursuit in future research on this topic.

Organizational versus individual goal integration mechanisms. We have dealt in this study with goal integration mechanisms as *organizational* processes or strategies for increasing the overlap between individual goals and organizational objectives. This should not be taken as implying that individuals are passive elements in the organization who do not employ a variety of their own strategies for increasing goal integration. In the first place, the individual decides which organizations he will join and may change his organizational affiliations frequently in an attempt to find one whose objectives are compatible with his personal goals. This self-selection process may be the ultimate goal integration mechanism viewed from the standpoint of the individual. Secondly, the individual may play an active role in the goal integration mechanisms we have presented and may be viewed as making use of complementary mechanisms to increase his goal integration with the organization. For example, any exchange relationship is a reciprocal one. The individual plays an active role in determining the terms of the exchange—he may offer more or less of his skills and energies to be used in pursuing organizational objectives in exchange for a given amount of organizational contribution to his personal goal attainment. Socialization might also be viewed in reverse—by persistently verbalizing and modeling his personal goals, the individual might succeed in getting the organization to adopt some of them as organizational objectives. Further, no organizational role is ever completely designed by the organization—an individual always participates to some extent in the design of his role, even if the organization makes no explicit attempt to design a role in terms of an individual's goals (cf. Levinson, 1959). These examples are intended to suggest that while the present study does not deal explicitly with goal integration from the individual's standpoint, this complementary view is an important one and might profitably be followed up in future investigations.

VI
Summary and Conclusions

The nature of the relationship between social organizations and their individual members has long been an issue of considerable interest to both students and administrators of organizations. This study represents an attempt to examine empirically one aspect of this general issue, namely the relationship of an organization's objectives to the goals of its individual members.

An *objective* is any state of affairs, static or dynamic, which contributes to the creation of an organization's primary outputs or to the fulfillment of its purposes or functions. A *goal* is any static or dynamic state of affairs which contributes to the fulfillment of an individual's needs, motives or desires. Organizations or sub-units whose members find it easy to attain personal goals and organizational objectives through the activities they engage in as members of the organization are said to have a high degree of *goal integration.*

Approaches used to increase the degree of goal integration in organizations may be classified into three broad categories or *goal integration models.* In the *exchange model,* a fairly explicit bargaining relationship prevails between the organization and the individual. The organization assists the individual in the pursuit of some of his personal goals and, in return, he devotes some of his time and energy to helping the organization pursue some of its specific objectives. Examples of particular *goal integration mechanisms* falling under the exchange model are the use of pay to encourage individuals to engage in activities that are not intrinsically interesting and the provision of social incentives, such as supportive relationships with superiors or the opportunity to interact informally with peers, *on the condition* that the individual is contributing to the achievement of organizational objectives.

Under the second general approach, called the *socialization model,* goal integration is achieved by influencing the individual to adopt some of the organization's objectives as personal goals or to give up personal goals that conflict with organizational objectives. Under this model, either a formal leader or members of a peer group may, through persuasion or example-setting, encourage the individual to adopt organizational objectives as personal goals. Thus we may speak of both leader socialization and peer socialization as particular mechanisms under the socialization model. Under the third approach, referred to as the *accommodation model,* the emphasis is on taking individual goals as given and attempting to design the roles and processes needed for attaining organizational objectives in such a way that these individual goals can be achieved. Particular mechanisms falling under this model include designing organizational roles or jobs with the needs and interests of their occupants in mind, and providing for participation of individuals in the objective-setting and problem-solving processes of the organization.

One major focus of this study concerned relationships between the use of the various mechanisms described above and the degree of goal integration achieved in organizational units. A second major focus concerned relationships between the degree of goal integration present and (1) the quality of functioning of organizational units as reflected in their communication, coordination and control processes, in their innovativeness and in their self-rated effectiveness, (2) reactions of individuals to their membership in the organization as reflected in their levels of motivation, satisfaction, commitment to the organization and freedom from job-related tensions.

Measures of the use of the various goal integration mechanisms, the degree of goal integration present in organizational units, the functioning of organizational units, and the reactions of individuals to their membership in the organization were collected by questionnaire from a total of 1,781 persons in a 2,800-employee oil refinery. Non-supervisory employees and employees from every level of management, representing each of the three major divisions of the refinery (Processing, Maintenance and Administration), were included in the study.

Results from the analysis of these questionnaire measures indicate that the degree of goal integration that exists in an organization or sub-unit is significantly associated with the quality of organizational functioning and with the way in which individuals react to their membership in the organization. More specifically, our data indicate that organizational units that rank high in goal integration also tend to rank high with regard to the amount of communication that occurs within them, the amount of influence exercised over the unit's activities by all levels of employees within the unit, the adequacy of coordination within the unit and between it and other units, and the number of innovative ideas that are generated for solving work problems. In addition, individuals who rank high in the extent to which they see their personal goals as being integrated with the organization's objectives also tend to rank high in their motivation to come to work and work hard, in their satisfaction with the organization and their job in it, and in their feelings of loyalty to the organization and commitment to its success. These results seem to justify the conclusion that the goal integration concept is a useful one, having demonstrated explanatory power with regard to a number of important variables describing behavior within organizations.

Goal integration mechanisms associated with the three general approaches or models described above differ in the strength of their relationships to the degree of goal integration present in organizational units. Mechanisms associated with the exchange model show inconsistent, generally low and sometimes negative relationships to the level of goal integration present. These exchange mechanisms, it appears, are clearly ineffective means of generating high levels of goal integration in organizations. Mechanisms associated with the socialization and accommodation models, on the other hand, reveal significant positive relationships to goal integration, with accommodation mechanisms showing the highest relationships of all. The use of socialization and accommodation mechanisms, therefore, would seem to be an effective means of generating high levels of goal integration in organizations.

In addition to differing in the overall strength of their relationships to goal integration, the three models also differ in terms of the stability of these relationships across units which differ in terms of the average education or tenure of their members, and in terms of whether their members are of predominately rural or urban background, are of managerial or non-managerial status, and are engaged in production work or in administrative and research activities. The accommodation model is the most stable of the three, showing approximately equal relationships to goal integration for units which differ on the demographic variables listed above. The socialization model is also fairly stable across units with different demographic characteristics, although some variation in effectiveness is apparent. For example, the socialization model relates more highly to goal integration in units which include a majority of members from rural backgrounds than in units whose members are of predominately urban background. The exchange model is the least stable of the three, showing wide variations in its relationship to goal integration across units which differ in their standing on the demographic variables considered here. To the extent that the exchange model has any positive effect on the level of goal integration achieved in an organization, this effectiveness appears to be limited to units whose members are of generally lower social or organizational status, that is, units with lower educational levels and non-managerial status.

Correlations among measures of the use of the three models indicate that the socialization and accommodation models tend to be used together in practice and that both tend to be essentially independent of the use of an exchange model. This suggests that socialization and accommodation models may belong to a single management system—i.e., a set of compatible management practices—while the exchange model belongs to a different management system. The socialization and accommodation models of goal integration appear to be compatible with the "participative" or "democratic" management systems proposed by a number of current organizational social psychologists (e.g., Argyris, 1964; Likert, 1961; McGregor, 1960), while the exchange model appears to be most compatible with the more restricted prescriptions of the "classical" or "traditional" organization theorists (e.g., Gulick and Urwick, 1937; Taylor, 1923; Weber, 1947).

The unconditional use of incentives—a set of management practices not included in any of our three goal integration models—was also examined in terms of its relation to the degree of goal integration present in organizational units and in terms of its association in practice with the use of our three models. This practice of providing material or social incentives without making their provision conditional upon any particular behavior of organization members seemed worth investigating because of its contrast to the kind of incentive provision implied by the exchange model, namely that the organization provides material or social incentives *on the condition* that the individual contributes to achieving the organization's objectives. In our data, the unconditional provision of incentives shows a significant positive relationship to goal integration and also tends to be associated in practice with the use of socialization and accommodation mechanisms. Unconditional provision of incentives is not related in practice to the use of exchange mechanisms. These results, together with those described in the preceding paragraph, suggest that the unconditional provision of incentives might be considered along with the use of socialization and accommodation mechanisms as an integral part of a participative management system. This appears to be a novel idea, since the participative management theorists mentioned above, while rejecting the particular practices associated with the exchange model, still discuss the use of incentives within a framework that assumes a conditional provision of incentives.

It appears reasonable to conclude from this study that the concept of goal integration has both theoretical and practical relevance and that our general theoretical model, which suggests a number of organizational processes leading to and a number of outcomes following from different degrees of goal integration, is a useful way of thinking about this issue. The question of the proper relationship between individual human beings and social collectivities is still very much with us in this age of increasing organizational life. It is hoped that continued development of theory and an expansion of empirical research efforts in this area will help us find creative answers to this vital question.

Appendix A
Detailed Description
of the Sample

A description of the sample in terms of some general characteristics appears in Table 20, which presents percentage distributions for sex, age, education and community background of the refinery employees included in this study. It is evident that few females are included; the refinery does not employ many women and secretarial and stenographic personnel were specifically excluded from the study. Respondents were relatively old; 65 per cent were over 45 years of age. The number of subjects in the lowest age bracket is somewhat lower in this sample than for the refinery as a whole due to the exclusion of apprentices from the present study. Relative frequencies in the other categories, however, are representative of the entire employee group. More than 80 per cent of the employees in this study have at least a high school education, a result in part of a policy introduced in the refinery several years ago to require a high school diploma for employment. Although the city in which the refinery is located continues to grow and the general area to urbanize, the background of most of the refinery's employees is rural or small-town. Less than one quarter of the employees included in this study were brought up in large cities or suburban areas.

A further description of the sample, based on some organizational characteristics, is presented in Table 21. This table contains data regarding the distribution of subjects across various tenure categories, hierarchical levels and functional specialties within the refinery. These data indicate that the employees of this refinery are not only a fairly old group, they are also characterized by a high proportion of long-service employees. Eighty-seven per cent of the employees have at least 16 years of service, with over 40 per cent having more than 25 years of service. If the apprentices were included, the

101

under five years of service category would have about twice as many employees as indicated here, but the bulk of the actual operating employees is still heavily concentrated in the high-tenure categories. There is about a 60-40 percentage split between non-supervisory employees and supervisory-managerial personnel, with first-line supervisors constituting almost three-fourths of the managerial group. Looking at the distribution across functions, it can be seen that about two-thirds of the employees perform what might be called the primary production work of the refinery, with the remaining one-third engaged in administrative or research and development activities. Within the production group, the ratio of maintenance personnel to refining equipment operators is about two to one.

Table 20

GENERAL CHARACTERISTICS OF SUBJECTS
N = 1,781

Sex		Education	
Male	96%	Less than high school graduate	17%
Female	4	High school graduate	37
		Some college	23
		College graduate	23
Total	100%	Total	100%
Age		**Background**	
Under 41 years	20%	Rural area or farm	40%
41-45 years	15	Town or small city	37
46-55 years	46	Suburban area near large city	12
Over 55 years	19	Large city	11
Total	100%	Total	100%

Table 21

ORGANIZATIONAL CHARACTERISTICS OF SUBJECTS
N = 1,781

Tenure	
Under 5 years	9%
5-15 years	4
16-25 years	43
Over 25 years	44
Total	100%

Hierarchical Level	
Top managers	2%
Middle managers	9
First line supervisors	31
Non-supervisory employees	58
Total	100%

Functional Specialty	
Continuous process production	23%
Mechanical maintenance and construction	44
Technical research and development	20
Staff and administration	13
Total	100%

Appendix B
Measures of Major Concepts

Questionnaire items used as measures of the major concepts investigated in this study are presented below, along with a description of how individual items relate to the concept being measured and an explanation of the index construction procedure when the procedure differs from those described in Chapter 3. Each individual questionnaire item is a specific question included in the April, 1968 survey. Most questions are answered on a five-point Likert-type scale, with the following set of answer alternatives:

(1) To a very little extent
(2) To a little extent
(3) To some extent
(4) To a great extent
(5) To a very great extent

Exceptions to this general pattern will be pointed out as the specific questions are presented below.

Measures of Goal Integration

Two different measures of the extent of goal integration present in an organizational unit are used in this study. The first is an index constructed from scores on the following two items.

To what extent is the company effective in getting you to meet its needs and contribute to its effectiveness?

To what extent does the company do a good job of meeting your needs and goals as an individual?

The first item above measures the individual's contribution to meeting the organization's objectives. The second item measures the organization's contribution to meeting the goals of the individual. Neither directly measures the concept of goal *integration,* so a special indexing procedure was used to combine scores on these two items. The formula for combining these scores can be stated in words as follows: first, take the lower of the scores on these two items and divide it by the higher of the two scores; then multiply this quotient by the mean of the two scores. The first operation provides a measure of how closely the two scores *match,* i.e., it indicates whether the individual's and the organization's needs are being met equally well, or whether one set of needs is being met more adequately than the other. The second operation introduces a measure of the average *level* of fulfillment of these two sets of needs. Reflected in the index score, then, are both the general level of fulfillment and the degree of congruence in fulfilling the organization's objectives and the individual's goals. When each set of needs is maximally fulfilled, the index score has its highest value (i.e., $5 \div 5 \times 5 = 5.00$). When one set of needs is maximally fulfilled and the other minimally fulfilled, the index score has its lowest value (i.e., $1 \div 5 \times 3 = 0.60$). When both sets of needs are fulfilled equally, but at a low level, the index score remains near the low end of the scale (e.g., $1 \div 1 \times 1 = 1$). Combining scores in this way makes the index a measure of goal *integration*, rather than merely an average of individual satisfaction from and contribution to the organization. At the same time, it assumes that the concept of goal integration refers to a congruence in *fulfillment* of goals and objectives, and that a situation of equally unfulfilled needs does not satisfy the definition of high goal integration.

A second measure of goal integration consists of the mean score on these two questionnaire items:

> If you devoted all your effort on the job to activities which directly satisfy your own personal needs and interests, to what extent would you be doing things which also help the company be successful?

> If you devoted all your effort on the job to activities which directly help the company be successful, to what extent would you be doing things which also satisfy your own personal needs and interests?

These questions pose two hypothetical situations for the respondent, and ask him to estimate the degree of goal integration that would occur under each. The first question seeks an estimate of the extent of goal integration that would be possible if he were to emphasize fulfilling his own goals on the job.

The second asks how much goal integration would be possible if his prime concern were always to help achieve the organization's objectives. In terms of Figure 1, the first question seeks an estimate of the size of subset C relative to the size of set A. The second questions seeks an estimate of the size of subset C relative to the size of set B. The index score, then, provides an estimate of the size of subset C relative to the combined sizes of sets A and B, or, in other words the extent to which his personal goals and the organization's objectives overlap.

To simplify some analyses and make the presentation of results less cumbersome, it was occasionally helpful to make use of a single measure of goal integration. For these purposes a summary goal integration index was created by taking the mean score on the two *indices* described above.

Measures of the Use of Exchange Mechanisms

Pay. The use of pay as an exchange mechanism was measured by the following single questionnaire item:

> To what extent are you paid for doing things which
> are not in themselves interesting to you?

Reliance on a single item in this instance reflects the difficulty that was experienced in trying to formulate measures of this concept. Because money is such a general symbol, its use can be conceived as an expression of many different approaches to goal integration. Formulating a measure that would incorporate the assumptions of the exchange model, and not be subject to alternative interpretations, proved to be no easy task. The above item focuses on the use of pay as an extrinsic motivator. In this way, it incorporates the assumption implicit in the exchange model that intrinsic motivation is impossible or very difficult to achieve, and that the most productive approach to goal integration is to provide extrinsic rewards that employees desire in exchange for the performance of work activities that employees, in the absence of external forces, would not desire to engage in.

Informal social relations. An index consisting of the mean score on the following two items measures the use of informal social relations as an exchange mechanism:

> When your supervisor shows an interest in your off-
> the-job activities, to what extent does he do this as a
> way of rewarding you for getting the work out?

> To what extent are informal conversations on the job
> permitted only when persons are performing their jobs
> well?

Two kinds of social incentives found by early human relations researchers to be important to employee motivation are tapped by these items—considerate treatment from superiors and opportunities for informal peer relations on the job. Here again, however, the emphasis is on making the provision of social conditions desired by the individual explicitly conditional upon the performance of activities that contribute to achieving the organization's objectives.

For analyses in which a single measure of the use of an exchange model was desired, a summary index was constructed by taking the mean score on the pay and informal social relations measures described above.

Measures of the Use of Socialization Mechanisms

Leader socialization. Use of this mechanism is measured by the mean score on these two questionnaire items:

> How much does your supervisor encourage people to give their best effort?

> To what extent does your supervisor maintain high standards of performance?

Peer socialization. The mean score on two items parallel to those above provide a measure of peer socialization:

> How much do persons in your work group encourage each other to give their best effort?

> To what extent do persons in your work group maintain high standards of performance?

These indices are intended to measure socialization by the leader or by peers through processes of persuasion, tapped by the first item in each set, and modeling, tapped by the second item in each set. They reflect the assumption of the socialization model that exposing individual members to these processes will cause them to internalize the organization's objectives—i.e., to adopt these objectives as personal goals.

A socialization model summary index was constructed by taking the mean score on the two indices described above.

Measures of the Use of Accommodation Mechanisms

Role design. A two-item mean-score index was used to measure the use of role design as an accommodation mechanism:

> In this company, to what extent are the interests and

needs of employees taken into account when jobs are designed or work activities are assigned?

To what extent is this company willing to change or give up work methods or objectives which go against the needs and interests of employees?

Participation. Use of this mechanism is measured by an index derived from scores on the following four items:

How are objectives set in this company?

(a) Objectives are announced with no opportunity to raise questions or give comments
(b) Objectives are announced and explained, and an opportunity is then given to ask questions
(c) Objectives are drawn up, but are discussed with subordinates and sometimes modified before being issued
(d) Specific alternative objectives are drawn up by supervisors, and subordinates are asked to discuss them and indicate the one they think is best
(e) Problems are presented to those persons who are involved, and the objectives felt to be best are then set by the subordinates and the supervisor jointly, by group participation and discussion

When decisions are being made, to what extent are the persons affected asked for their ideas?

When your supervisor has problems related to the work, to what extent does he use group meetings to talk things over with his subordinates and get their ideas?

How often does your supervisor hold group meetings where he and the people who work for him can really discuss things together?

The first two items in the above list were originally combined into a mean-score index called "consultative decision-making," with the second two items similarly combined and labeled "group problem-solving." While a distinction between these two concepts can be made and may sometimes be important, for our purposes the concepts are similar enough and their measures highly enough related ($r = .42$ across 1,781 individuals) to justify combining them into a single measure. The participation index, therefore, was constructed by taking the mean score on these two sub-indices.

Both the role design and the participation measures reflect the accommodation model's emphasis on taking individual goals as given and designing the roles and processes needed for attaining organizational objectives in such a way that these individual goals can be achieved.

An accommodation model summary index will be used in some analyses. It consists of the mean score on the role design and participation indices.

Measures of Department Functioning

Four separate measures of the functioning of departmental units in the refinery were constructed from questionnaire items included in the 1968 survey. Items selected for this purpose were ones which either referred directly to some aspect of department functioning, or which referred to a unit more general than the immediate work group and dealt with processes that seemed to offer reasonable bases for differentiating departments.

Communication. A mean-score index composed of the following two items was used to measure this aspect of department functioning:

> How hard do people try to see that their supervisor and his superiors get full and accurate information about work problems?

> People at all levels of a company usually have know-how that could be of use to decision-makers. To what extent is information widely shared in this company so that those who make decisions have access to all available know-how?

Neither of these items refers directly to the department as the unit whose functioning is being described. In fact, the second item has as its referent "the company." In spite of this, it was thought possible to use these items to assess the functioning of departments, so long as the data were aggregated by department. The assumption required here is that each employee's impression regarding upward communication attempts and the sharing of information in the company are determined primarily by his experiences in his own organizational unit. Differences in department mean scores on these items, then, are assumed to represent real differences in communication processes between departments.

Coordination. Interdepartmental coordination was measured by the mean score on these two items:

> To what extent do persons in different departments plan together and coordinate their efforts?

> In working with other departments, problems are
> bound to arise from time to time. When these prob-
> lems do occur, to what extent are they handled well?

Total influence. Both this and the following measure of department
functioning were constructed from a composite questionnaire item dealing
with influence exercised over department activities:

> In general, how much say or influence does each of
> the following groups of people have on what goes on
> in your *department?*
>
> (a) Lowest-level supervisors (foremen, office super-
>   visors, etc.)
> (b) Top managers (president, vice presidents, heads of
>   large divisions, etc.)
> (c) Employees (people who have no subordinates)
> (d) Middle managers (department heads, area
>   managers, etc.)

Response alternatives for each part of this composite question consisted of a
five-point scale running from "little or no influence" to "very great influence." A measure of the total amount of influence exercised within the
department was constructed by taking the mean score on parts (a), (c), and
(d) of this question. Similar measures of total influence have been used in a
number of organizational studies and have been found to consistently relate to
measures of organizational effectiveness (cf. Tannenbaum, 1968).

Influence distribution. A simple measure of the distribution of influence
within a department was constructed by subtracting the score on part (c) of
the composite influence question presented above from the score on part (d)
of that question. The index score, then, represents the difference between the
amount of influence the department head is seen as exerting over department
affairs and the amount of influence non-supervisory employees are seen as
having over these affairs. The larger the score on this index, the more influence is concentrated in the hands of the department head. The smaller the
score, the more equal the distribution of influence between the top and
bottom levels within the department. Such difference scores have also been
used in the influence studies mentioned above. While they have not exhibited
such consistent relationships to organizational effectiveness as have the total
influence measures, the concept of influence distribution seemed interesting
enough to justify including such a measure in this study.

Measures of Work Group Functioning

Four measures of the functioning of work group units in the refinery were constructed from questionnaire items. A work group unit consists of a set of individuals who report to the same immediate superior.

Interaction. The general level of interaction among members of a work group was assessed by a mean-score index of the following two questions:

> To what extent do persons in your work group keep each other informed about important events and situations?

> To what extent do persons in your work group exchange opinions and ideas?

Coordination. This aspect of work group functioning was measured by the mean score of these two items:

> To what extent do persons in your work group provide the help you need so that you can plan, organize, and schedule work ahead of time?

> To what extent do members of your work group plan together and coordinate their efforts?

Innovation. Activities within the work group directed toward creating new work methods or new solutions to job problems were assessed by the mean score on these two items:

> To what extent do persons in your work group help you find ways to do a better job?

> To what extent do persons in your work group offer each other new ideas for solving job-related problems?

Effectiveness. The overall effectiveness of a work group's functioning, as seen by its members, was measured by this two-item mean-score index:

> To what extent does your work group make good decisions and solve problems well?

> On the basis of your experience and information, how would you rate your work group on effectiveness? How well does it do in fulfilling its mission or achieving its goals in comparison with other work groups in the company?

Self-rating measures of the effectiveness of organizational units, similar to the second item above, have been shown to relate strongly to similar ratings made of these units by members of higher management. Neither self nor superior ratings of work group effectiveness are as desirable as measures that require little or no judgment, such as measures of physical output quantity. Since no such measures were available for work groups in, the refinery, however, the above index was deemed worthy of inclusion in this study.

Measures of Individual Reactions

Reactions of individuals to their membership in the organization were measured by means of the four two-item mean-score indices presented below.

Motivation. An item tapping general attraction to the work place and one dealing with forces toward a high level of work effort were combined to provide an index of individual motivation:

> How much do you look forward to coming to work each day?

> To what extent are there things about working here (people, policies, or conditions) that encourage you to work hard?

Satisfaction. Items concerned with the most general and most specific aspects of satisfaction with organizational membership were incorporated into a general measure of individual satisfaction:

> All in all, how satisfied are you with this company, compared to most others?

> All in all, how satisfied are you with your job?

Commitment. A measure of felt responsibility for the organization's success and a measure of felt loyalty were combined to form an index of the individual's commitment to the organization.

> To what extent do you feel a real responsibility to help the company be successful?

> To what extent do you have a feeling of loyalty toward this company?

Health reactions. Two measures of job-related tension were combined into a general measure of the effect of organizational membership on the health of individuals:

To what extent do you find it difficult to sleep at night because you keep thinking of what happened at work during the day?

To what extent does your job make you feel nervous and "jumpy"?

These two items are adaptations of items used in a national sample survey of mental health (Gurin, Veroff, and Feld, 1960).

Appendix C
Formula for Testing the Significance
of a Difference Between Taus

The formula for the normal deviate associated with a difference between two taus, used in performing the significance tests for Tables 10 and 17, was derived in the manner described below. It involves combining the basic logic for testing the significance of a difference between two sample means (cf., e.g., McNemar, 1969, p. 114) with the formula for computing the variance of the tau statistic (cf. Siegel, 1956, p. 221). The author is grateful to Andrew Stedry of the Department of General Business at the University of Texas for assistance in deriving this formula.

1. Basic formula for the normal deviate associated with a difference between two sample means:

$$z = \frac{\text{Difference Between Means}}{\text{Standard Deviation of the Difference}} = \frac{M_1 - M_2}{\sqrt{S^2_{M_1} + S^2_{M_2}}}$$

2. Substituting taus for means and using Siegel's formula for the variance of tau:

$$z = \frac{T_1 - T_2}{\sqrt{\dfrac{2(2N_1 + 5)}{9N_1(N_1 - 1)} + \dfrac{2(2N_2 + 5)}{9N_2(N_2 - 1)}}}$$

115

3. Adding weights to the variances of the two sample taus to correct for unequal N's:

$$z = \frac{T_1 - T_2}{\sqrt{\left(\frac{N_1}{N_1 + N_2}\right) \frac{2(2N_1 + 5)}{9N_1(N_1 - 1)} + \left(\frac{N_2}{N_1 + N_2}\right) \frac{2(2N_2 + 5)}{9N_2(N_2 - 1)}}}$$

4. Simplifying and combining terms produces the following formula, which was used in computing the normal deviate associated with differences between pairs of taus:

$$z = \frac{T_1 - T_2}{\sqrt{\frac{2[(2N_1 + 5)(N_2 - 1) + (2N_2 + 5)(N_1 - 1)]}{9(N_1 + N_2)(N_1 - 1)(N_2 - 1)}}}$$

References

Andrews, F. M., Morgan, J. N. and Sonquist, J. A. *Multiple classification analysis*. Ann Arbor: Survey Research Center, Institute for Social Research, 1967.

Argyris, C. The individual and organization: some problems of mutual adjustment. *Administrative Science Quarterly*, 1957, *2*, 1-24.

Argyris, C. *Integrating the individual and the organization*. New York: John Wiley and Sons, Inc., 1964.

Barnard, C. *The functions of the executive*. Cambridge, Massachusetts: Harvard University Press, 1938.

Bendix, R. and Fisher, L. H. The perspectives of Elton Mayo. In A. Etzioni (Ed.), *Complex organizations: A sociological reader*. New York: Holt, Rinehart and Winston, 1961, pp. 113-126.

Bennis, W. G. *Changing organizations*. New York: McGraw-Hill, 1966.

Blake, R. R. and Mouton, J. S. *The managerial grid*. Houston, Texas: Gulf, Publishing, 1964.

Blau, P. *Exchange and power in social life*. New York: John Wiley & Sons, Inc., 1964.

Blood, M. R. and Hulin, C. L. Alienation, environmental characteristics, and worker responses. *Journal of Applied Psychology*, 1967, *51*, 284-290.

Bowers, D. G. and Seashore, S. E. Predicting organizational effectiveness with a four-factor theory of leadership. *Administrative Science Quarterly*, 1966, *11* (2), 238-263.

Etzioni, A. *Modern organizations*. Englewood Cliffs, New Jersey: Prentice-Hall, Inc., 1964.

Fiedler, F. E. *A theory of leadership effectiveness*. New York: McGraw-Hill, 1967.

Fleishman, E. A. Leadership climate, human relations training, and supervisory behavior. *Personnel Psychology*, 1953, *6*, 205-222.

Gulick, L. and Urwick, L. (Eds.). *Papers on the science of administration*. New York: Institute of Public Administration, 1937.

Gurin, G., Veroff, J., and Feld, S. *Americans view their mental health.* New York: Basic Books, 1960.

Herzberg, F. *Work and the nature of man.* Cleveland: World Publishing Company, 1966.

Homans, G. C. Social behavior as exchange. *American Journal of Sociology,* 1958, *63*, 597-606.

Katz, D. and Kahn, R. L. *The social psychology of organizations.* New York: John Wiley and Sons, Inc., 1966.

Katzell, R. A. Contrasting systems of work organization. *American Psychologist,* 1962, *17*, 102-108.

Leavitt, H. J., and Whisler, T. L. Management in the 1980's. *Harvard Business Review,* 1958, *36* (6), 41-48.

Levinson, D. J. Role, personality, and social structure in the organizational setting. *Journal of Abnormal and Social Psychology,* 1959, *58*, 170-180.

Likert, R. *The human organization: its management and value.* New York: McGraw-Hill, 1967.

Likert, R. *New patterns of management.* New York: McGraw-Hill, 1961.

McGregor, D. *The human side of enterprise.* New York: McGraw-Hill, 1960.

McNemar, A. *Psychological statistics.* New York: John Wiley and Sons, Inc., 1969.

Maier, N. R. F. and Hoffman, L. R. Organization and creative problem-solving. *Journal of Applied Psychology,* 1961, *45*, 277-280.

March, J. G. and Simon, H. A. *Organizations.* New York: John Wiley and Sons, Inc., 1958.

Metcalf, H. and Urwick, L. (Eds.). *Dynamic administration, the collected papers of Mary Parker Follett.* New York: Harper, 1942.

Porter, L. W. Job attitudes in management: I. Perceived deficiencies in need fulfillment as a function of job level. *Journal of Applied Psychology,* 1962, *46*, 375-384.

Porter, L. W. and Lawler, E. E. Properties of organization structure in relation to job attitudes and job behavior. *Psychological Bulletin,* 1966, *66*, 235-251.

Roethlisberger, F. J. and Dickson, W. J. *Management and the worker.* Cambridge, Massachusetts: Harvard University, 1939. Paperback edition: Science Editions, John Wiley and Sons, Inc., New York, 1964.

Rousseau, J. J. *The social contract.* New York: Hofner, 1949.

Schein, E. H. Management development as a process of influence. *Industrial Management Review,* 1961, *1*, 55-97.

Schein, E. H. *Organizational psychology.* Englewood Cliffs, New Jersey: Prentice-Hall, Inc., 1965.

Schein, E. H. *Organizational socialization and the profession of management.* Cambridge, Massachusetts: Massachusetts Institute of Technology, 1967.

Siegel, S. *Nonparametric statistics.* New York: McGraw-Hill, 1956.

Simon, H. A. *Administrative behavior.* (2nd ed.) New York: Mcmillan, 1957. Paperback edition: Free Press, New York, 1965.

Simon, H. A. Comments on the theory of organizations. In A. H. Rubenstein and C. J. Haberstroh (Eds.), *Some theories of organization.* Homewood, Illinois: Dorsey Press and Richard D. Irwin, 1960, pp. 157-167.

Simon, H. A. On the concept of organizational goal. *Administrative Science Quarterly,* 1964, *9* (1), 1-22.

Strauss, G. The personality vs. organization theory. In L. R. Sayles, *Individualism and big business.* New York: McGraw-Hill, 1963, pp. 67-80.

Strauss, G. Some notes on power-equalization. In H. Leavitt (Ed.) *The social science of organizations: four perspectives.* Englewood Cliffs, New Jersey: Prentice-Hall, Inc., 1963, pp. 41-84.

Tannenbaum, A. S. *Control in organizations.* New York: McGraw-Hill, 1968.

Taylor, F. W. *The principles of scientific management.* New York: Harper, 1923.

Viteles, M. S., Wilson, A. T. M., and Hutte, H. A. Personality and organization: the individual and the system: A symposium. In G. Nielson (Ed.), *Proceedings of the XIV International Congress of Applied Psychology, Vol. 5. Industrial and business psychology.* Copenhagen: Munksgaard, 1962, pp. 97-115.

Vroom, V. H. The effects of attitudes on the perception of organizational goals. *Human Relations,* 1960, *13,* 229-240.

Weber, M. *The theory of social and economic organization.* (Translated by A. M. Henderson and T. Parsons.) T. Parsons (Ed.). New York: Free Press, 1947.

Wilson, T. P. Patterns of management and adaptations to organizational roles. A study of prison inmates. *American Journal of Sociology,* 1968, *74* (2), 146-157.